Elvis
A CELEBRATION IN PICTURES

Elvis

A CELEBRATION IN PICTURES

Charles Hirshberg
and the Editors of

LIFE

WARNER BOOKS

A Time Warner Company

ACKNOWLEDGMENTS

THE AUTHOR WISHES TO THANK THE ENTIRE STAFF OF LIFE MAGAZINE FOR UNFLAGGING HELP, ENTHUSIASTIC ENCOURAGEMENT AND GOOD-NATURED TOLERANCE. SPECIAL THANKS TO ADRIENNE AURICHIO, WHO COLLECTED THE PHOTOGRAPHS FOR THIS BOOK, AND TO TOM BENTKOWSKI AND MIMI PARK, WHO WORKED MAGIC WITH THEM. EXTRA-SPECIAL THANKS TO SETH GODDARD AND STEPHANIE H. O'BRIEN, PEERLESS RESEARCHERS NOW EXPERT IN ALL ASPECTS OF PRESLEYANA. JAY LOVINGER, PATRON SAINT OF NERVOUS WRITERS, PROVIDED PATIENT EDITING AND, WHEN NECESSARY, OUTPATIENT PSYCHOTHERAPY. NIKKI AMDUR, ROBERT ANDREAS, SUSAN BOLOTIN, SUSAN SUFFES AND ROBERT SULLIVAN ALSO HELPED EDIT THE MANUSCRIPT. LAWRENCE P. BRACKEN SUPERVISED THE TECHNICAL ASPECTS OF THE PROJECT, ALBERT RUFINO WAS A WORKHORSE ON THE COPY DESK, AND PAMELA SZTYBEL WINNINGHAM ASSISTED IN PHOTO RESEARCH. THANKS ALSO TO MARILYN LIPSIUS AND ERNST MIKAEL JØRGENSEN OF BMG MUSIC. FINALLY, A 21-GUN SALUTE TO DANIEL OKRENT, CAPTAIN OF THE GOOD SHIP LIFE, WHO PROVIDED A STEADY HAND ON THE TILLER AND AN EVEN STEADIER SENSE OF HUMOR.

A NOTE ON SOURCES

THE FOLLOWING FRIENDS AND ASSOCIATES OF ELVIS PRESLEY ASSISTED IN THE PREPARATION OF THIS BOOK: CHET ATKINS, ANITA AND HELEN CARTER, JUNE AND JOHNNY CASH, BARBARA EDEN, D.J. FONTANA, MARY JENKINS, TINA LOUISE, SCOTTY MOORE, DR. GEORGE NICHOPOULOS, SAM PHILLIPS, LINDA THOMPSON, RED WEST. THREE EXCELLENT BOOKS ALSO PROVED INDISPENSABLE: ROSE CLAYTON AND DICK HEARD'S **ELVIS UP CLOSE**; ELAINE DUNDY'S **ELVIS AND GLADYS**; AND PETER GURALNICK'S **LAST TRAIN TO MEMPHIS**. ALSO CONSULTED: **ELVIS AND ME**, BY PRISCILLA BEAULIEU PRESLEY WITH SANDRA HARMON; AND **ELVIS: WHAT HAPPENED?** BY RED WEST, SONNY WEST AND DAVE HEBLER WITH STEVE DUNLEAVY.

PICTURE SOURCES ARE LISTED BY PAGE.

COVER: POSTER COURTESY RCA RECORDS LABEL.
12: AP/WIDE WORLD PHOTOS.
14: BOTTOM, COLIN ESCOTT COLLECTION.
16: MICHAEL OCHS ARCHIVES.
28: LEFT, MICHAEL OCHS ARCHIVES;
RIGHT, ARCHIVE PHOTOS.
42: LEFT, ARCHIVE PHOTOS;
RIGHT, MICHAEL OCHS ARCHIVES.
51: TOP, PAUL LICHTER'S ELVIS ARCHIVES;
BOTTOM, BETTMANN/UPI.
93: M-G-M. 94-95: EVERETT COLLECTION (26);
THE KOBAL COLLECTION (2);
MOTION PICTURE & TV PHOTO ARCHIVE (3).
96: PARAMOUNT PICTURES.
98-99: ARCHIVE PHOTOS (1); BETTMANN/UPI (2);
EVERETT COLLECTION (8); M-G-M (1);
MOTION PICTURE & TV PHOTO ARCHIVE (1);
PARAMOUNT PICTURES (1); PHOTOFEST (10).
104: BETTMANN/UPI.
112: LEFT, PHOTOFEST; RIGHT, MICHAEL OCHS ARCHIVES.
113: CLOCKWISE FROM TOP LEFT, PHOTOREPORTERS;
FOTOS INTERNATIONAL/ARCHIVE PHOTOS;
RON GALELLA; EVERETT COLLECTION;
DAGMAR/SHOOTING STAR;
MOTION PICTURE & TV PHOTO ARCHIVE;
GLOBE PHOTOS; RON GALELLA; CENTER, GLOBE PHOTOS.
114: PHIL ROACH/PHOTOREPORTERS.

DESIGNED BY TOM BENTKOWSKI & MIMI PARK
PHOTO EDITING BY ADRIENNE AURICHIO

WARNER BOOKS, INC.
1271 AVENUE OF THE AMERICAS
NEW YORK, NY 10020

○ A TIME WARNER COMPANY

PRINTED IN THE UNITED STATES OF AMERICA
FIRST PRINTING: SEPTEMBER 1995
10 9 8 7 6 5 4 3 2 1

ISBN: 0-446-52020-9
LC: 95-61093

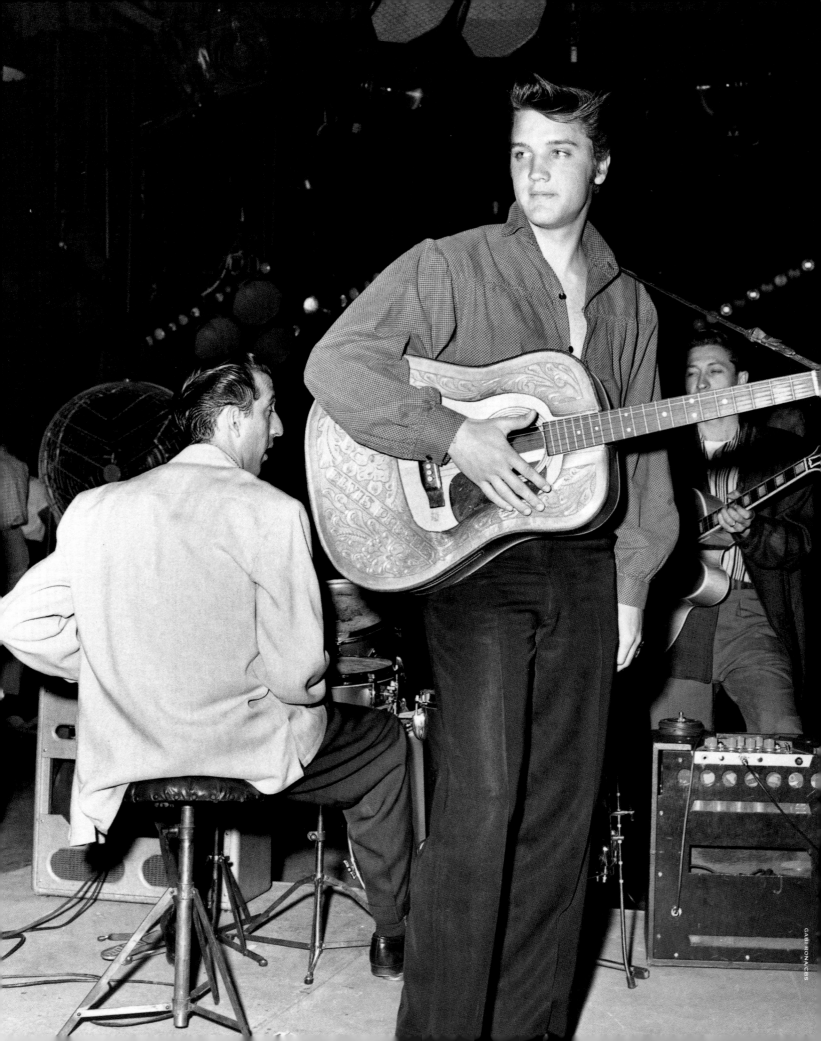

Let us begin with a confession: This is not the first book ever published on the subject of Elvis Presley.

There are, in fact, so many that anyone who ventures to write a new one ought to have a damn good reason.

Fortunately, the reason for this one is pretty obvious: LIFE magazine and Elvis Presley go together like ice cream and pie. Both belong to the American landscape almost as much as Mount Rushmore. Both belong to the same generation, too: Elvis was born in January of 1935 and LIFE in November of the following year. And most important, Elvis was one of the most photogenic individuals who ever lived.

It's a good thing too, for even Elvis's most devoted fans will agree that the King's unsurpassed genius for self-expression lay in his art, not in his speech. True, he could carry off anything from a libidinous mating call like "A Big Hunk O' Love" to a sacred testimonial like "His Hand in Mine"; he could, in fact, say more just by curling his lip or swiveling his pelvis than most politicians can say in a dozen harangues. But for the past two decades, biographers have been scavenging yellowed news clippings and transcripts of obscure press conferences, as well as the memories of Elvis's friends, hoping to find some grand soliloquy or trenchant self-analysis he may have left behind. (Another confession: We tried too.) Such searches are probably futile. Elvis Presley devoured his time on earth, and it devoured him. It was almost as if his mouth was too full of the spice of life for him to talk much about it.

Fortunately, he left behind something far better than words: a story, or if you like, a legend. And when told in pictures, this story becomes a spectacle of matchless force—as you will soon see.

So that's the reason for this book, but it gives rise to another question: If LIFE and Elvis are so perfect together, why wasn't it published a long time ago?

One more confession. For many years, LIFE had a blind spot about rock and roll in general and Elvis in particular. It would have been odd indeed if Henry Luce—the patrician founder of LIFE, and of Time Inc., a man of firm and passionate beliefs—had dug the King. He did not, and neither did his magazine, which early on depicted Elvis as a reasonably congenial weirdo ("a 21-year-old hillbilly who howls, mumbles, coos and cries") who had the potential to become a moral menace ("he uses a bump and grind routine usually seen only in burlesque").

Well . . . sorry. But America has changed a bit in the intervening years. At this writing, Elvis would have been 60 and, had he lived, he, too, would have been surprised to see moms and dads attending Rolling Stones concerts with their children—to say nothing of teenagers with nose rings snapping their fingers to the strains of Tony Bennett. Rest assured, LIFE has seen the light.

One thing more should be noted in the old LIFE's defense: it was the first national magazine to cover Elvis at all. And though its words were unworthy of both it and the King, its pictures were quite the opposite. They were rich and sensuous and, at the same time, wonderfully simple—like ice cream and pie.

Taste for yourself.

—Charles Hirshberg

IT WAS A TRAGIC AND GLORIOUS DAY WHEN THE TWINS ARRIVED. TRAGIC BECAUSE THE FIRST, JESSE GARON, WAS DEAD. HIS FATHER PLACED THE TINY CORPSE IN A SHOE BOX AND BURIED IT IN AN UNMARKED GRAVE. GLORIOUS BECAUSE THE SECOND, ELVIS ARON, WAS BOUND FOR GREATNESS, HIS MOTHER WAS SURE. "WHEN ONE TWIN DIES," SHE LATER TOLD ELVIS, "THE ONE WHO LIVES GETS THE STRENGTH OF BOTH."

JANUARY 8

1935

ELVIS'S FIRST PERFORMING TRIUMPH CAME AT THE AGE OF 10, TWO YEARS PRIOR TO THIS PORTRAIT. THE OCCASION WAS CHILDREN'S DAY AT TUPELO'S MISSISSIPPI-ALABAMA FAIR AND DAIRY SHOW. STANDING ON A CHAIR TO REACH THE MIKE, HE SANG "OLD SHEP," A MAUDLIN BALLAD ABOUT A BOY AND HIS FAITHFUL DOG: "IF DOGS HAVE A HEAVEN, THERE'S ONE THING I KNOW/OLD SHEP HAS A WONDERFUL HO-O-O-ME." ELEVEN YEARS LATER, HE WOULD RECORD THE SONG FOR RCA.

Unable to hold a steady job, Vernon Presley decides to move the family to Memphis. The city is steeped in music: There is blues on Beale Street, country on the radio and gospel everywhere—especially at the Poplar Street Mission, across the street from the Lauderdale Courts housing project, where the Presleys live. Elvis makes friends with Johnny and Dorsey Burnett, two future rockabilly stars, and the three spend many evenings jamming in the project's laundry room.

He is born in a two-room shotgun shack in East Tupelo, Miss. Though Elvis's great-uncle Noah Presley is elected mayor of the town shortly after Elvis's birth, the family is so poor that the doctor who delivers Elvis eventually collects his fee from a welfare agency.

For his 11th birthday, Elvis receives the most important gift of his life—a guitar. Soon he is bringing it with him to school almost every day, singing for his friends at lunchtime, talking dreamily about the *Grand Ole Opry*. On one occasion, bullies swipe it and cut the strings.

PREVIOUS PAGE:
CATASTROPHE AWAITED ELVIS, TWO, AND HIS PARENTS, GLADYS AND VERNON. NOT LONG AFTER THIS PICTURE WAS TAKEN, VERNON WAS CONVICTED OF FORGERY (THE ALTERED CHECK WAS WORTH LESS THAN $5); HE SPENT EIGHT MONTHS AT MISSISSIPPI'S INFAMOUS PENITENTIARY, PARCHMAN FARM. GLADYS AND ELVIS WERE EVICTED FROM THEIR HOME SHORTLY AFTER VERNON WAS TAKEN AWAY.

13

A FAINTLY MUSTACHIOED ELVIS AND THE SO-CALLED BLUE MOON BOYS, GUITARIST SCOTTY MOORE (LEFT) AND BASSIST BILL BLACK (RIGHT), HUNG OUT IN 1954, NOT LONG AFTER ONE OF THE GREAT RECORDING SESSIONS IN ROCK HISTORY. IT HAD BEGUN UNSPECTACULARLY, WITH ELVIS CROONING A COUPLE OF BALLADS FOR PRODUCER SAM PHILLIPS. THEN, DURING A BREAK, HE LAUNCHED INTO "THAT'S ALL RIGHT (MAMA)." PHILLIPS FLIPPED. "HEY, WHAT ARE YOU DOING?" HE HOLLERED FROM THE CONTROL ROOM. "WE DON'T KNOW," THEY REPLIED. "WELL, BACK UP," SAID PHILLIPS, "AND DO IT AGAIN!"

A recent high school graduate (he excelled at shop), Elvis is employed at M.B. Parker Machinists' Shop when he walks into Memphis Recording Service to make a record at his own expense. The receptionist, Marion Keisker asks, "Who do you sound like?" "I don't sound like nobody," he replies. After hearing Elvis sing, she is sufficiently impressed to note his name with this comment: *Good ballad singer.*

Sam Phillips, the proprietor of both Memphis Recording Service and Sun Records, invites Elvis to try to record something for commercial release. Elvis labors through a song called "Without You," and though Phillips is disappointed, he introduces the kid to guitarist Scotty Moore and bass player Bill Black. He asks Elvis to rehearse with them and to return a week or so later.

Sun Records releases Elvis's first single. Side one offers a countrified version of a blues song—Arthur "Big Boy" Crudup's "That's All Right (Mama)." Side two features a rhythm-and-bluesy version of a country song (Bill Monroe's "Blue Moon of Kentucky"). Country deejays say it's too bluesy, and R&B deejays say it's too country. But a few pioneers, like Memphis deejay Dewey Phillips (no relation to Sam), hear in it something wild and new—rock and roll—and so do their listeners.

A COUNTRY
BOY ROCKED
CLEVELAND: ELVIS
AT BROOKLYN
HIGH SCHOOL IN
THE FALL OF '55.

Elvis's boyhood dream of appearing on the *Grand Ole Opry* comes true. Naturally, he is nervous—the more so since *Opry* star Bill Monroe is rumored to be less than flattered by Presley's version of "Blue Moon of Kentucky." ("I'd heard he was going to break my jaw," Sam Phillips would later say.) But Monroe is polite and stoic. Unfortunately, so is the audience.

Elvis receives a far more enthusiastic reception at the *Louisiana Hayride,* Shreveport, La.'s answer to Nashville's *Opry.* Says country star Porter Wagoner: "Elvis would throw his guitar around over his shoulder, and then Bill Black would try and do that with his big stand-up bass. People would tear the house down!" In a month, Elvis is headlining the show.

D.J. Fontana, former house drummer for the *Louisiana Hayride,* officially joins Elvis's band. Fontana has experience playing for exotic dancers outside of Shreveport, where he would pound his tom-toms in time to their gyrations. He applies the same technique whenever he sees Elvis "scooting across the stage," and Elvis loves it. This, Fontana speculates, "is why I got the job."

NINETEEN FIFTY-FOUR WAS ELVIS'S LAST YEAR OF INNOCENCE. HE BEGAN IT AS A TRUCK DRIVER AND ENDED IT AS AN UP-AND-COMING "HILLBILLY" SINGER. HE CONTINUED TO TAKE HIS HOMETOWN SWEETHEART, DIXIE LOCKE, FOR MILK SHAKES, AND TO LISTEN TO RECORDS FROM CHARLIE'S RECORD SHOP ON NORTH MAIN STREET. HE WAS SOPHISTICATED ABOUT ONLY ONE THING— MUSIC. AT RIGHT, HE ADMIRED AN OBSCURE R&B RECORD ON THE KING LABEL.

17

HE WAS NEVER SO TERRIFIED AS THE DAY HE WALKED

ONSTAGE AT THE OVERTON PARK SHELL IN MEMPHIS, JULY 30,

1954. THE PEOPLE HAD COME TO HEAR SLIM WHITMAN CROON

"INDIAN LOVE CALL." BUT FIRST THEY GOT ELVIS. AS SOON AS

HE BEGAN TO SING, THEY BEGAN TO HOOT. THEY'RE MAKING

FUN OF ME, HE THOUGHT. DEVASTATED, HE FINISHED "BLUE

MOON OF KENTUCKY" AND SLUNK OFF. BUT BACKSTAGE EVERY-

ONE WAS ELATED, PUSHING HIM OUT FOR AN ENCORE. *THE*

GIRLS LOVE YOU, THEY TOLD HIM. *IT'S THE WAY YOU SHAKE!*

MAKING OF A STAR

He best day of his life may have been when he returned to Tupelo wearing the velvet shirt he'd been given by Natalie Wood. The town greeted him with a huge "welcome home" banner and he performed for 5,000 screaming fans. One was 14-year-old Wynette Pugh—better known today as Tammy Wynette.

It was a time when hair was short, suits were made of gray flannel and sex was rarely on public display. A lot of people liked it that way—and hated Elvis. "The spirit of Presleyism has taken down all morals," preached Rev. Carl E. Elgena of Des Moines. Psychiatrist Richard Hoffman lamented from his Park Avenue office: "Instead of honoring names like Carlyle, the average child in New York knows all about Presley." At first, Elvis tried to explain. "I watch my audiences and I listen to them," he said. "I know that we're all getting something out of our system, but none of us knows what it is." Eventually, he gave up trying to put it into words.

BETTMANN/UPI (5)

A GAGGLE OF
ELVIS ADMIRERS IN
AMARILLO, TEX.,
GETTING SOMETHING
OUT OF THEIR SYSTEM.

24

A.Y. OWEN

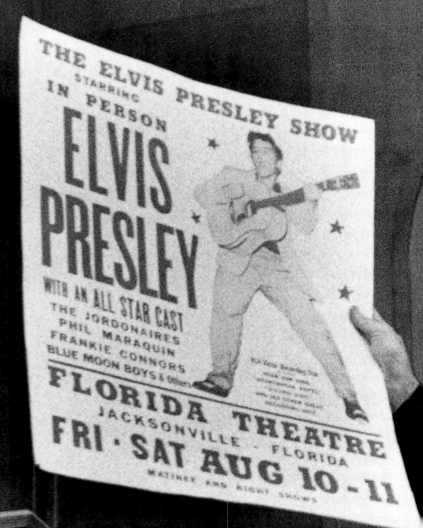

26

The controversy over Elvis's sex appeal reached its zenith during the summer of '56, when Elvis arrived in Jacksonville, Fla., for a series of performances. When he had appeared there in 1955, the Jacksonville girls had been so impressed they'd risen as one to strip him of his clothes. Now, in an effort to protect these females from further enjoyment, the Reverend Robert Gray held a prayer meeting at Trinity Baptist Church. There he informed his teenage flock that Elvis Presley had "achieved a new low in spiritual degeneracy. If he were offered his salvation tonight, he would probably say, 'No thanks.'" The teens were then instructed to bow their heads and pray for Elvis's redemption. When Elvis learned of this, he was deeply insulted. "I feel the preacher was just looking for publicity," he said. "I have gone to church since I could walk,"

W

HILE
REVEREND GRAY
PRAYED FOR ELVIS'S
SOUL, JACKSONVILLE
JUDGE MARION
GOODING THREATENED
TO ARREST HIS BODY
ON OBSCENITY
CHARGES. "DON'T
UNDERESTIMATE THE
INTELLIGENCE OF
TEENAGERS IN SEXUAL
MATTERS," WARNED
HIS HONOR. "THEY
CAN READ ALL THAT
STUFF." ELVIS MET
WITH GOODING,
PROMISED TO BEHAVE
AND THEN DROVE THE
JACKSONVILLE GIRLS
WILD BY WAGGING HIS
FINGER SUGGESTIVELY
WHILE SINGING.
"DRIVE CAREFUL ON
YOUR WAY HOME," HE
TEASED THE CROWD.
"AND DON'T LET
ANYBODY PASS YOU."

Burdened by debts,
Sam Phillips sells
Elvis's Sun contract
to RCA Victor for the
unheard-of sum of
$35,000, plus
$5,000 for back
royalties. It's a
career-risking bet
by RCA executive
Steve Sholes.

The Elvis Presley
Jamboree, managed
by Colonel Parker,
kicks off in Texas.
The bill includes
future stars
Floyd Cramer and
Johnny Cash.

Elvis makes his
national television
debut on *Stage
Show,* produced by
Jackie Gleason and
hosted by the Dorsey
brothers. Gleason's
opinion: "He can't
last. I tell you flatly,
he can't last."

The first national
magazine to do a
story on Elvis is
LIFE—which
describes him as a
"howling hillbilly."

Dressed in tails, he
appears on Steve
Allen's *Tonight* show
and sings "Hound
Dog" to a top-hatted
basset hound
named Sherlock.

DON WRIGHT

| OCTOBER 1955 | NOVEMBER 1955 | JANUARY 1956 | APRIL 1956 | JULY 1956 |

29

FAN MAIL CAN BE TIRING, ESPECIALLY WHEN YOU GET AN AVERAGE OF 10,000 LETTERS A WEEK. FOR SOME MYSTERIOUS REASON, ELVIS DEVELOPED THE HABIT OF RIPPING THEM UP AFTER READING THEM. IN THIS CASE, PRIOR TO AN APPEARANCE ON CBS's *STAGE SHOW*, HE LEFT THE TORN REMNANTS ON THE COFFEE TABLE.

As his career gathered the momentum of a train 16 coaches long, Elvis became increasingly insecure. "I'm afraid to wake up each morning," he confessed. "I can't believe all this has happened to me. I just hope it lasts."

ROBERT W. KELLEY

I**N THE STUDIO HE COMBINED UNBRIDLED PASSION WITH RELENTLESS PROFESSIONALISM. HE RECORDED "HOUND DOG" IN 1956 (LEFT)—AND RECORDED IT AND RECORDED IT. THIRTY-ONE TAKES LATER HE WAS FINALLY SATISFIED.**

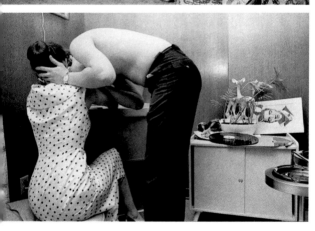

B Y 1956 THE PRESLEY FAMILY HAD WHAT THEY'D ALWAYS WANTED: A RANCH-STYLE DREAM HOUSE IN AN UPPER-MIDDLE-CLASS MEMPHIS NEIGHBORHOOD. THERE, ELVIS DOTED ON HIS MOTHER, WHO TOLD A FRIEND THAT IF ELVIS WOULD ONLY RETIRE FROM MUSIC AND BUY A FURNITURE STORE, SHE WOULD BE "THE HAPPIEST PERSON IN THE WORLD." ELVIS WAS DOTING ON YOUNGER WOMEN TOO, LIKE BARBARA HEARN. FRESH FROM THE SHOWER, HE ROCKED WITH BARBARA TO THE STRAINS OF "DON'T BE CRUEL" (OPPOSITE, TOP), CLINCHED WITH HER TO "ANY WAY YOU WANT ME" (CENTER), THEN TRIED TO PERSUADE HER TO KEEP BOPPIN' AND LORD KNOWS WHAT ELSE (BOTTOM). WHEN SHE DECLINED— PERHAPS BECAUSE GLADYS WAS HOVERING IN A NEARBY ROOM—HE SULKED (LEFT).

35

In Memphis, Independence Day 1956 was also Elvis Presley Day by proclamation. Seven thousand fans came to hear him at a benefit. Angered by demeaning treatment he had been subjected to on the *Tonight* show, many rushed the stage to welcome him home. "Those people in New York are not gonna change me none," he promised. "I'm gonna show you the real Elvis tonight."

THE ROCK AND ROLL CIRCUIT OF THE '50S WAS A MIX OF GLITZ AND GRIND. ON THE ONE HAND, ELVIS AND HIS ENTOURAGE TRAVELED IN THIS LAVENDER CONTINENTAL. ON THE OTHER, THEY TRAVELED ALL NIGHT, FROM ONE GIG TO ANOTHER. HERE, THEY ARRIVED IN NEW ORLEANS AFTER DRIVING 557 MILES STRAIGHT FROM JACKSONVILLE. THE FUTURE KING TOOK HIS TURN AT THE WHEEL LIKE EVERYONE ELSE. "WE SHARED EVERYTHING IN THOSE DAYS," ONE MEMBER OF THE ENTOURAGE RECALLED WISTFULLY. "EVEN WOMEN."

THERE WAS ALWAYS A BUZZ OF EXPECTATION IN THE CROWDS THAT ASSEMBLED BEFORE ELVIS'S SHOWS. COLONEL PARKER MADE SURE OF IT BY KEEPING BOX OFFICES CLOSED AS LONG AS POSSIBLE, SO FANS HAD NOTHING TO DO BUT MILL AROUND AND GROW INCREASINGLY IMPATIENT AND EXCITED. BUT THESE CROWDS WERE OUTDONE BY THE FRENZIED MOBS THAT SURROUNDED ELVIS BACKSTAGE AFTER THE SHOWS ENDED. COUNTRY SINGER HELEN CARTER, WHO TOURED WITH HIM ALONG WITH HER MOTHER AND SISTERS, RECALLED ONE NIGHT WHEN "THE CROWD PUSHED ONE LITTLE GIRL CLEAN BACK INTO OUR DRESSING ROOM. WE SAID, 'NOW, HONEY, WE'LL LET YOU OUT THE BACK SO YOU CAN GO TO YOUR CAR.' BUT SHE CRIED, 'I CAN'T! MY MAMA'S IN THERE TRYING TO KISS HIM!'"

ROBERT W. KELLEY

Elvis drops by Sun
Studios and spends
an evening jamming
with Carl Perkins and
Jerry Lee Lewis. Elvis
is particularly
impressed with
Lewis: "The way he
plays piano just
gets inside me."
Johnny Cash shows
up later and is
photographed with
the trio, giving rise to
the myth of a Million
Dollar Quartet.

He finally appears on
*The Ed Sullivan
Show*. But in one
of TV's most
notorious—and
frustrating—acts of
censorship, his
spectacular gyrations
are shown only from
the waist up.

Elvis purchases a
custom pink Cadillac
Fleetwood for
Mama Gladys. (It's
still on display at
Graceland.)

N OTHING COMPARED
TO THE NOISE OF THOSE
SCREAMING GIRLS,"
RECALLS FORMER LIFE
CORRESPONDENT
(AND LATER MANAGING
EDITOR) RICHARD
STOLLEY, WHO COVERED
ELVIS'S FLORIDA TOUR
IN 1956 (OPPOSITE).
"IT WAS UNEARTHLY;
IT HURT YOUR EARS."
THEIR SHRIEKING WAS
LESS AGONIZING TO
ELVIS, BUT BEFORE ONE
CONCERT IN RICHMOND,
VA., THEY STOOD
OUTSIDE THE WINDOW
AND SCREECHED SO
LOUDLY HE COULD
HARDLY HEAR EITHER
HIMSELF OR THE
JORDANAIRES, HIS
BACKUP VOCAL GROUP.

© ALFRED WERTHEIMER

S INCE
REPORTERS HAD
NEVER ENCOUNTERED
ANYTHING LIKE
ELVIS BEFORE, MOST
DIDN'T QUITE KNOW
WHAT TO ASK HIM.
WAS IT TRUE THAT
HE ONCE SHOT HIS
MOTHER?, THEY
WANTED TO KNOW.
WAS IT TRUE HIS
MOVEMENTS ON STAGE
WERE THE RESULT OF
MARIJUANA USE?
WAS IT TRUE HE
RECEIVED A CUT FROM
THE SALE OF "I HATE
ELVIS" BUTTONS?
HE ANSWERED ALL
SUCH QUESTIONS WITH
UNFAILING SOUTHERN
POLITENESS—"NO,
SIR," "NO, MA'AM"
AND "WELL, I BELIEVE
THAT ONE TAKES
THE CAKE."

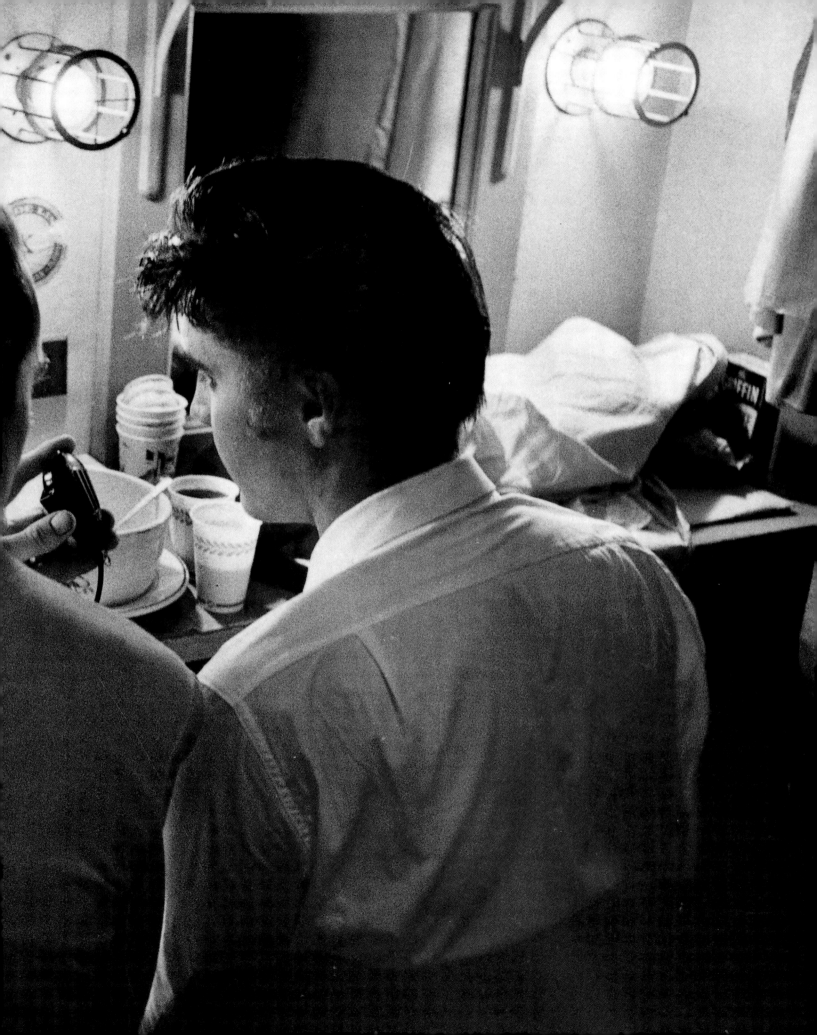

E

LVIS SEEMS TO COME ALIVE ONLY WHEN A GIRL IS AROUND," REPORTER KAYS GARY NOTED. IN A STAIRWELL AT THE RICHMOND CONCERT, HE CAME ALIVE WITH ONE HE HAD KNOWN FOR A VERY SHORT TIME. GARY ONCE SAW HIM IN A RESTAURANT, FLIRTING WITH WOMAN AFTER WOMAN. "HE STOOD CHEST-TO-CHEST WITH ONE, RUNNING HIS FINGERS LIGHTLY AROUND THE BLOUSE RUFFLES. AND SHE STOOD STILL AND SAID NOTHING WHILE HE TALKED TO HER IN A LOW VOICE." WHEN HE MET A WOMAN HE LIKED, IT WAS NOT UNCOMMON FOR HIM TO REACH OUT AND TOUCH HER SKIRT OR CRANE HIS NECK TO NIBBLE HER FINGER. SAID CLOSE FRIEND AND BODYGUARD RED WEST: "THAT BOY SURE HAD A CONSTITUTION IN THOSE EARLY DAYS."

I'LL REGRET THIS DAY AS LONG AS I LIVE," HE SAID ON OCTOBER 19, 1956. THE TROUBLE BEGAN WHEN HE DROVE HIS WHITE CONTINENTAL MARK II INTO A MEMPHIS SERVICE STATION RUN BY ONE EDD HOPPER. A CROWD FORMED AROUND THE CAR, AND HOPPER, OUTRAGED THAT OTHER PAYING CUSTOMERS COULDN'T REACH HIS PUMPS, ORDERED HIM TO MOVE. "I'M FIXIN' TO," ELVIS SAID, BUT HE WAS HEMMED IN AND HAD NOWHERE TO GO. SO HOPPER REACHED IN AND SWATTED HIM ON THE BACK OF THE HEAD. ELVIS BOLTED FROM HIS CAR AND SOCKED HOPPER IN THE EYE. ("THAT EYE LOOKED LIKE A TRAVELING BAG," ONE WITNESS REMARKED.) THE NEXT DAY IN COURT, ELVIS WAS EXONERATED AND HOPPER (NEAR RIGHT, IN SUNGLASSES) FINED $26. BUT ELVIS HAD MADE AN OMINOUS DISCOVERY: HE WAS NO LONGER FREE TO ACT LIKE A NORMAL PERSON IN PUBLIC. "IT'S GETTING WHERE I CAN'T EVEN LEAVE THE HOUSE," HE SIGHED.

Almost as soon as he hit the big time, Elvis began to assemble a gang of friends, relations and sycophants that came to be known as the Memphis Mafia. One important task was helping Elvis warm up, or cool down, with gospel harmonies between shows. Here, Red West (center) did his duty with Jordanaires Hoyt Hawkins (far left) and Hugh Jarrett.

Elvis purchases his mansion, Graceland. A bubble-gum maker wants to strip the wood paneling off the walls of Elvis's old house, saw it into pieces, then sell it like baseball cards—with gum. Because this would conflict with other deals he has made, the Colonel declines.

Elvis appears for the first time in his fabulous gold lamé suit designed by Nudie, a Brooklyn-born former boxer who had honed his sartorial skills by making costumes for burlesque dancers.

The night before he reports for induction into the U.S. Army, Elvis hosts a private blowout at Memphis's Rainbow Rollerdrome. Dividing his friends into two teams, he gives the signal, and each side tries to knock the daylights out of the other.

| MARCH 1957 | MARCH 1957 | MARCH 1958 |

In September of 1957, Elvis got the shock of his life: The original Blue Moon Boys, guitarist Scotty Moore and bassist Bill Black, up and left him. He felt betrayed but shouldn't have. Scotty (near right) had played a crucial role in developing the unique fusion of blues and country known as the Presley Sound, but as Elvis had gotten richer, Scotty and Bill's share grew steadily smaller. They were put on salary instead of receiving a percentage of the profits and had been granted only one raise in two years. It was grossly unfair, but, according to Scotty, Elvis "kept saying he left the business side of it to Parker." Some weeks after their resignation, Scotty and Bill were offered a flat rate for each show. Reluctantly, they agreed. "Of course it stuck in my craw," said Scotty, who continued to play with Elvis off and on until 1969. "But we were still making more money than we could if we were driving trucks or something."

52

JOE RIMKUS

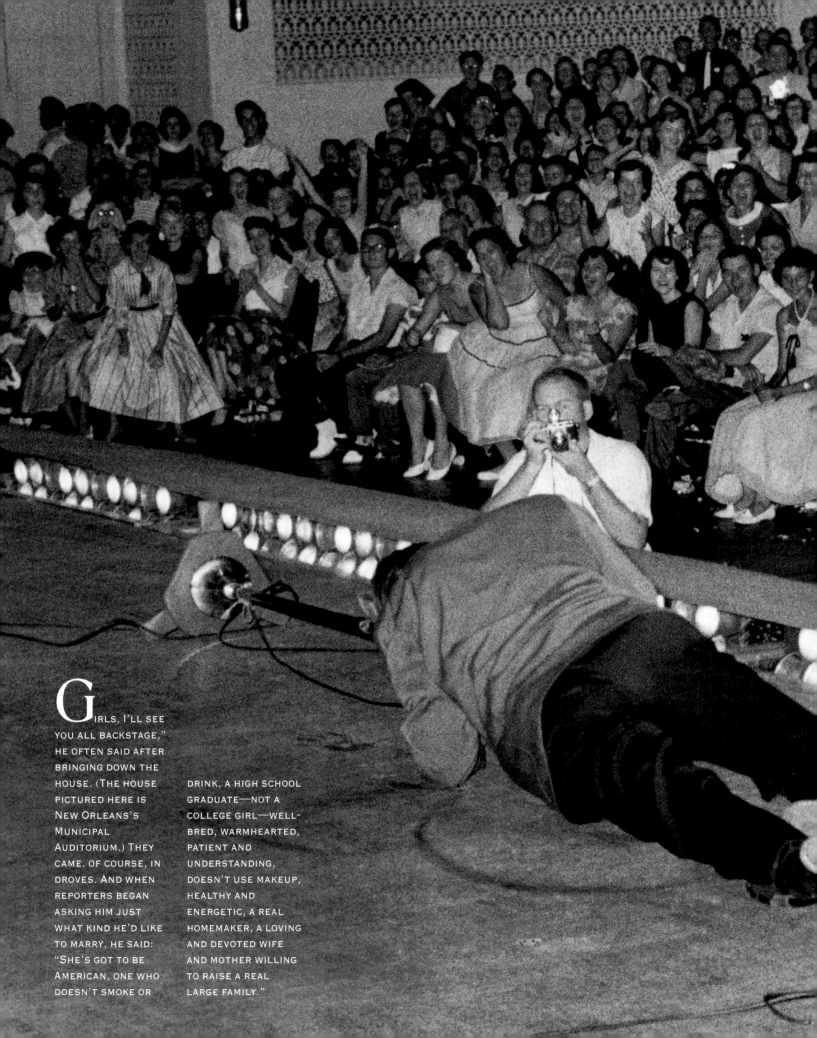

"GIRLS, I'LL SEE YOU ALL BACKSTAGE," HE OFTEN SAID AFTER BRINGING DOWN THE HOUSE. (THE HOUSE PICTURED HERE IS NEW ORLEANS'S MUNICIPAL AUDITORIUM.) THEY CAME, OF COURSE, IN DROVES. AND WHEN REPORTERS BEGAN ASKING HIM JUST WHAT KIND HE'D LIKE TO MARRY, HE SAID: "SHE'S GOT TO BE AMERICAN, ONE WHO DOESN'T SMOKE OR DRINK, A HIGH SCHOOL GRADUATE—NOT A COLLEGE GIRL—WELL-BRED, WARMHEARTED, PATIENT AND UNDERSTANDING, DOESN'T USE MAKEUP, HEALTHY AND ENERGETIC, A REAL HOMEMAKER, A LOVING AND DEVOTED WIFE AND MOTHER WILLING TO RAISE A REAL LARGE FAMILY."

55

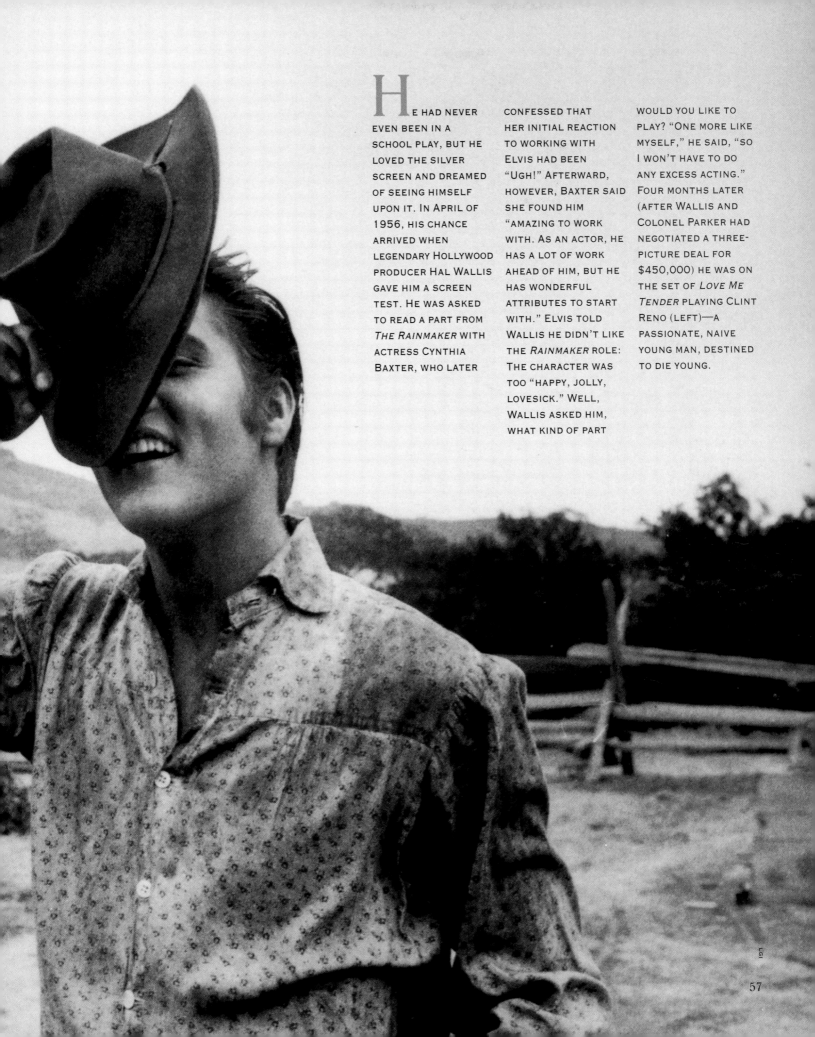

He had never even been in a school play, but he loved the silver screen and dreamed of seeing himself upon it. In April of 1956, his chance arrived when legendary Hollywood producer Hal Wallis gave him a screen test. He was asked to read a part from *The Rainmaker* with actress Cynthia Baxter, who later confessed that her initial reaction to working with Elvis had been "Ugh!" Afterward, however, Baxter said she found him "amazing to work with. As an actor, he has a lot of work ahead of him, but he has wonderful attributes to start with." Elvis told Wallis he didn't like the *Rainmaker* role: The character was too "happy, jolly, lovesick." Well, Wallis asked him, what kind of part would you like to play? "One more like myself," he said, "so I won't have to do any excess acting." Four months later (after Wallis and Colonel Parker had negotiated a three-picture deal for $450,000) he was on the set of *Love Me Tender* playing Clint Reno (left)—a passionate, naive young man, destined to die young.

57

H OW MUCH MAGNETISM DID ELVIS PRESLEY HAVE? IN 1958, SOPHIA LOREN SAW HIM FOR THE FIRST TIME IN THE PARAMOUNT COMMISSARY AND ASSAULTED HIM LIKE ANY OTHER GROUPIE.

H

E IS NOT MY CUP OF TEA," SAID ED SULLIVAN, AND INDEED IT IS HARD TO IMAGINE TWO SHOWMEN MORE UNALIKE THAN ELVIS AND ED. BUT WHEN THE PUBLIC DEMANDED IT, SULLIVAN OFFERED ELVIS A BOOKING ON HIS SHOW. COLONEL PARKER (LEFT, WITH THE STARS) STUNNED SULLIVAN BY DEMANDING A $50,000 FEE. THIS WAS 10 TIMES WHAT HAD BEEN OFFERED AND, IN FACT, MORE THAN ANYONE HAD EVER BEEN PAID FOR A TV APPEARANCE. STILL, SULLIVAN SWALLOWED HIS PRIDE AND SIGNED ELVIS FOR THREE SHOWS. GOOD MOVE: MORE THAN 80 PERCENT OF AMERICA TUNED IN TO THE FIRST PERFORMANCE. BY THE THIRD, SULLIVAN'S CONVERSION WAS COMPLETE. "THIS IS A REAL DECENT, FINE BOY," HE SAID. "WE'VE NEVER HAD A PLEASANTER EXPERIENCE WITH A BIG NAME."

E LVIS
CROONED (PROBABLY
"I WANT YOU, I NEED
YOU, I LOVE YOU") AND
CONCENTRATED AT
ONE OF HIS FIRST
SESSIONS FOR RCA IN
NASHVILLE. CHET
ATKINS PLAYED GUITAR
WHILE GORDON STOKER
AND BEN AND BROCK
SPEER ADDED
BACKGROUND VOCALS.
ELVIS WAS SHOELESS,
ATKINS LATER SAID,
BECAUSE "HE HAD SPLIT
HIS PANTS AND HAD TO
CHANGE 'EM. A
RECEPTIONIST FOUND
THE OLD ONES—THEY
WERE PINK AND BLUE
AND BLACK—AND
ASKED, 'WHAT DO YOU
WANT ME TO DO WITH
THESE?' I SAID, 'YOU
BETTER SAVE 'EM. HE'S
GONNA BE THE BIGGEST
THING EVER.' SHE KINDA
TURNED UP HER NOSE.
BUT TWO OR THREE
MONTHS LATER SHE
WAS TRYING TO GET
ON *I'VE GOT A SECRET*
BECAUSE SHE HAD
ELVIS'S PANTS."

DON CRAVENS (5)

62

A

T AN EXHAUSTING
RECORDING SESSION
IN NEW YORK
CITY, ELVIS
DISAPPEARED INTO
AN IMPENETRABLE
WORLD AS HE
LISTENED TO A DEMO
BY SONGWRITER OTIS
BLACKWELL. ALFRED
WERTHEIMER, WHO
PHOTOGRAPHED A
NUMBER OF RCA
SINGERS, WAS STRUCK
BY ELVIS'S FOCUS—
"HE HELD HIS
FOREHEAD IN HIS
HAND AND
CONCENTRATED ON
THE SOUND"—AND HIS
LEADERSHIP. "HE
NEVER CRITICIZED
ANYONE. HE'D JUST
SAY, 'O.K., FELLAS, I
GOOFED.'" BUT THERE
WAS NO GOOFING THIS
TIME: BLACKWELL'S
SONG WAS CALLED
"DON'T BE CRUEL."
LESS THAN A WEEK
AFTER ITS RELEASE,
WITH "HOUND DOG"
ON THE FLIP SIDE,
IT WAS ON THE BRINK
OF GOING GOLD.

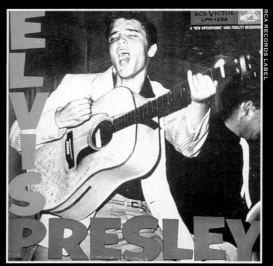

1956

THE BETTER TO DISPLAY HIS

COLLECTION OF GOLD AND

PLATINUM RECORDS, HE BUILT AN

80-FOOT HALLWAY AT GRACELAND. NOWADAYS, TOUR

GUIDES LOVE TO TELL VISITORS THAT MORE THAN A

BILLION ELVIS RECORDINGS HAVE BEEN SOLD. LAID END

TO END, THE GUIDES LIKE TO SAY, THESE WOULD CIRCLE

THE EARTH TWICE. THIS NEVER FAILS TO AMAZE.

PICTURED HERE ARE
THE COVERS
OF ALL OF ELVIS'S
ALBUMS— EXCEPT
GREATEST HITS
COLLECTIONS, BUDGET
KNOCKOFFS AND
OTHER REGURGITATIONS
OF THESE ORIGINALS.

1957

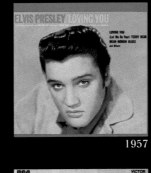

1957

1957

IN 1957, WHEN SOME
CONSIDERED CHRISTMAS
AND ROCK POLAR
OPPOSITES, *ELVIS'
CHRISTMAS ALBUM* WAS
BANNED BY MANY RADIO
STATIONS. SINCE THEN,
IT HAS SOLD MORE THAN
THREE MILLION COPIES.

1960

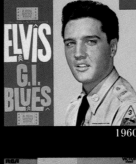

1960

1960

1961

19

1963

1964

1964

1965

19

1967

ELVIS WON HIS FIRST
GRAMMY FOR *HOW GREAT
THOU ART* IN 1967.
ALL THREE OF HIS
GRAMMYS WERE FOR
GOSPEL RECORDINGS.

1967

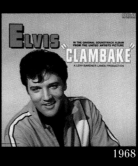

1968

19

1970

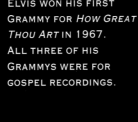

1970

1971

1971

19

1973

1973

ELVIS PRESLEY (PAGE 66)
WAS RCA'S FIRST POP
ALBUM CERTIFIED
AS A GOLD RECORD BY THE
RECORDING INDUSTRY
ASSOCIATION OF AMERICA.

1974

19

1958   1958   1959   1959

...MONTHS AFTER
...SE OF *BLUE*
...T HAD SOLD
...ES THAN
...EY ALBUM
...T TIME—
...ON.

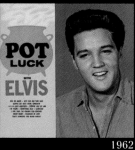    

1962   1962   1963

SO FAR, ELVIS HAS 61
GOLD AND PLATINUM
ALBUMS, MORE THAN
ANY OTHER ARTIST.
THE ROLLING STONES
ARE SECOND WITH 34.

1965   1966   1966

1968   1968   1969   1969

IN THE FOUR MONTHS
AFTER HIS DEATH, AN
ESTIMATED 200 MILLION
ELVIS RECORDS WERE
SOLD WORLDWIDE.

1972   1972   1972

ACCORDING TO *THE
OFFICIAL PRICE GUID...
ELVIS PRESLEY REC...
AND MEMORABILIA*, ...
ORIGINAL COPY OF H...
FIRST LP, *ELVIS PRE...*
IS WORTH FROM $8 T...
$300; HIS LAST, *MO...*

WHEN THE DRAFT NOTICE CAME, ALL HIS FRIENDS TRIED T

CHEER HIM UP. "ELVIS, THEY'LL NEVER TAKE YOU," CLIF

GLEAVES SAID. "YOU'RE TOO BIG." BUT IT WASN'T JUS

UNCLE SAM WHO WANTED HIM TO GO. SO DID COLONE

PARKER. THE DRAFT WAS A FREE PUBLIC-RELATION

BONANZA. WHEN THE ARMY OFFERED ELVIS A PERFORMER'

POST IN SPECIAL SERVICES, THE COLONEL WOULD HAVE NON

OF IT. "IF THEY WANT MY BOY TO SING," HE SAID, "THEY AR

GOING TO HAVE TO PAY FOR IT LIKE ANYONE ELSE." ELVIS'

AST WORDS AS A CIVILIAN WERE "F... CLIFF GLEAVES!

W

HY ME?" HE HAD
WEPT IN THE LAP OF
HIS OLD FRIEND
BARBARA PITTMAN A
FEW DAYS BEFORE
REPORTING FOR
INDUCTION IN MARCH
OF 1958. HE SAW NO
REASON TO BELIEVE
THERE WOULD BE
ANYTHING LEFT OF HIS
CAREER WHEN HIS
TWO YEARS OF GI
BLUES WERE DONE.
WORSE, HIS MOTHER,
GLADYS (TOP LEFT,
WEEPING), WHOM HE
LOVED ABOVE ALL
ELSE, WAS SUFFERING
MIGHTILY FROM
HEPATITIS, AND HE
COULDN'T BEAR TO
LEAVE HER. FOR THREE
DAYS, A MEDIA PARADE
WITH COLONEL TOM
AS GRAND MARSHALL
FOLLOWED ELVIS
THROUGH THE
INDUCTION PROCESS
(BOTTOM LEFT:
PARKER BREAKFASTING
WITH ELVIS SHORTLY
BEFORE HIS TRIP TO
THE ARMY BARBER).
THE PRESS HAD
ALWAYS MADE MUCH
OF ELVIS'S HAIR (*TIME*
REPORTED THAT IT
SWAM WITH "SWEAT
AND GOOSE GREASE"),
AND FLASHBULBS
POPPED LIKE MAD
DURING HIS SHEARING.
"I KNOW A LOT OF
PEOPLE WHO WOULD
PAY A LOT OF MONEY
FOR THAT HAIR!" THE
COLONEL CROWED.

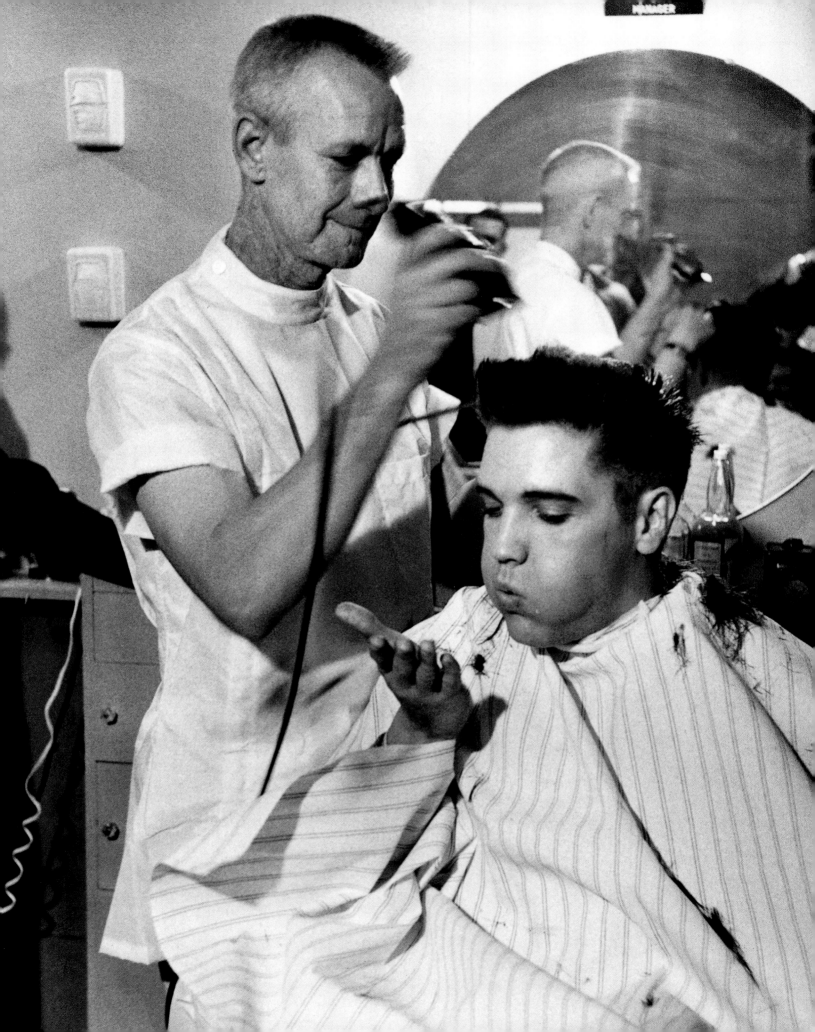

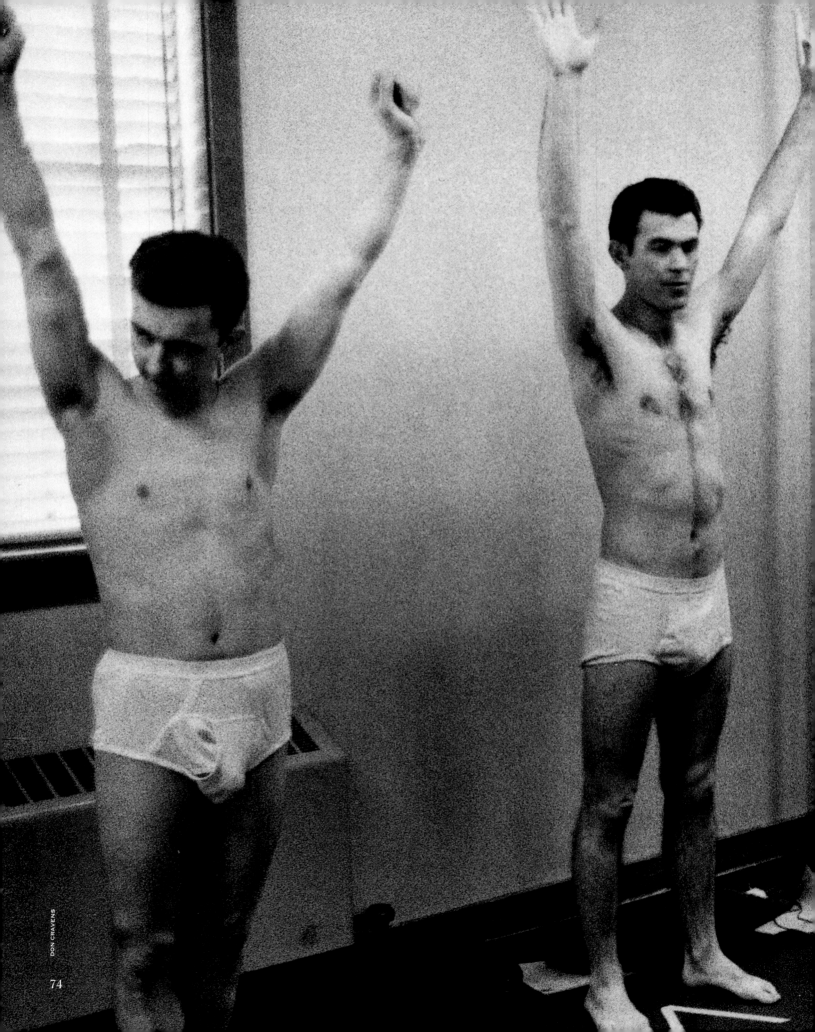

IF I SEEM NERVOUS," HE SAID BEFORE DOFFING HIS NAVY BLUE TROUSERS, GRAY-AND-WHITE CHECKED SPORT COAT, STRIPED SHIRT AND PINK-AND-BLACK SOCKS, "IT'S BECAUSE I AM."

After completing his physical at Kennedy Veteran's Hospital in Memphis, Elvis somberly kissed his parents (as well as a girlfriend or two) and took one last loving look at his Cadillac. "Goodbye, you long black sonofabitch," he told the car. The other inductees laughed, and Elvis boarded a bus for Fort Chaffee, Ark., where he was issued a pair of size 12 army boots (opposite) along with the rest of his military togs. Meanwhile, Colonel Parker, who had followed along with the pack of reporters, seemed happier than ever. He chatted with Army brass (top right) and newshounds (bottom right) and even handed out balloons advertising Elvis's new film, *King Creole*. One photographer actually hid in the barracks hoping for a shot of Elvis in his bunk, but the Army threw him out. King Elvis had become Private Presley.

"**M**ISS YOUR TEDDY BEAR, ELVIS?" THE OTHER SOLDIERS CHIDED HIM SHORTLY AFTER HE WAS POSTED TO FORT HOOD, TEX. ACTUALLY, IT WAS GLADYS WHOM HE MISSED. AS SOON AS HE COULD GET OFF BASE, HE RETREATED TO HIS OLD FRIEND EDDIE FADAL'S HOUSE IN WACO TO CALL HER. "FOR A SOLID HOUR, THEY WERE CRYING, WEEPING, MOANING ON THE TELEPHONE," FADAL RECALLED. "NOT HARDLY A WORD WAS SPOKEN." BUT LIKE MOST PRIVATES, ELVIS BEGAN TO GROW ACCUSTOMED TO ARMY LIFE. THE MEN BEGAN TO ACCEPT HIM, TOO. IT DIDN'T HURT THAT HE BOUGHT EVERYONE IN HIS UNIT A SPARE UNIFORM AND SOMETIMES PAID AS MUCH AS 20 BUCKS TO HAVE SOMEONE TAKE KP DUTY IN HIS STEAD. THEN, ON AUGUST 11, HE RECEIVED TERRIFYING NEWS: GLADYS'S HEALTH HAD TAKEN A TURN FOR THE WORSE. THOUGH HE WAS DUE FOR OVERSEAS POSTING IN SIX WEEKS, HE WAS GRANTED AN EMERGENCY FURLOUGH TO SEE HER.

S HE'S ALL I LIVED FOR," ELVIS WAILED. "SHE WAS ALWAYS MY BEST GIRL." WEARING A WHITE FRILLED SHIRT HIS DEAD MOTHER HAD OFTEN ADMIRED, HE SAT WITH HIS FATHER ON THE STEPS OF GRACELAND AND CRIED INCONSOLABLY (RIGHT), RISING ONLY TO BURY HIMSELF IN THE ARMS OF VISITING LOVED ONES. THEN, HE WOULD LEAD THESE FRIENDS AND RELATIONS TO HIS MOTHER'S OPEN COFFIN AND GENTLY STROKE HER CORPSE. "WAKE UP, MAMA," HE WHIMPERED. "WAKE UP, BABY, AND TALK TO ELVIS." WHEN HER BODY WAS LAID IN ITS GRAVE, HE TRIED TO LEAP IN AFTER IT. FOR DAYS, HE CLUTCHED HER PINK HOUSECOAT TO HIS BREAST AND KISSED IT LOVINGLY. ONE WITNESS CALLED IT "THE MOST PITIFUL SIGHT YOU EVER SAW."

A MONTH LATER AT BROOKLYN ARMY TERMINAL, HE STOOD BEFORE 125 REPORTERS (OPPOSITE), POLITE AND CHARMING AS EVER. HE ANSWERED ALL THE USUAL QUESTIONS IN THE USUAL WAY: NO, HE DIDN'T THINK HIS MUSIC CAUSED JUVENILE DELINQUENCY AND, NO, HE WASN'T ENGAGED TO BE MARRIED. BUT WHEN ASKED ABOUT HIS MOTHER, HE STRUGGLED TO EXPRESS HIS FEELINGS. "I WAS AN ONLY CHILD, AND MOTHER WAS ALWAYS RIGHT WITH ME," HE SAID. "I COULD WAKE HER UP ANY HOUR OF THE NIGHT IF I WAS WORRIED OR TROUBLED." HE WOULD NEVER SELL GRACELAND, HE ADDED, "BECAUSE THAT WAS MY MOTHER'S HOME." IN TRUTH, ELVIS NEVER RECOVERED FROM GLADYS'S DEATH. "HE CHANGED COMPLETELY," SAID LILLIAN MANN SMITH, AN AUNT WHO HAD KNOWN HIM FROM CHILDHOOD. "HE DIDN'T SEEM LIKE ELVIS EVER AGAIN."

BILL RAY

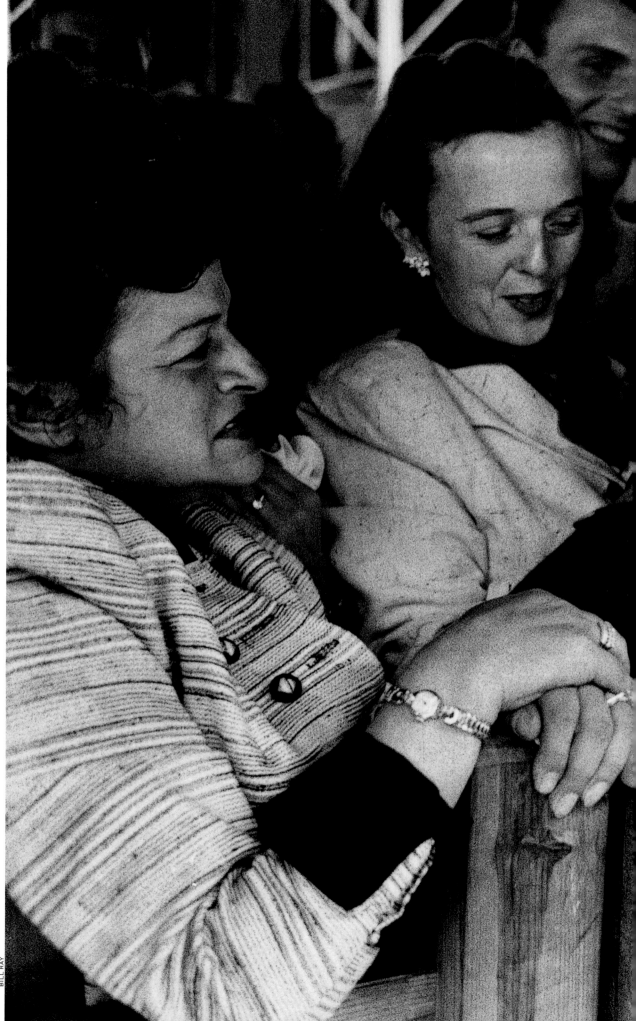

Although 2,000 yearning fans showed up at the Brooklyn pier (right) to see him off, Elvis's departure was far more excruciating for him than it was for them. Once again Colonel Parker and the media turned the event into a carnival. As photographers held their cameras at the ready and a military band played a brassy version of "Tutti Frutti," Elvis was ordered up the gangplank eight times carrying a duffel bag that wasn't even his. Finally, as the band struck up "Don't Be Cruel," the USS *General Randall* set sail for Germany. But for many nights after, Elvis's bunkmate, Charlie Hodge, lay in the ship's dark hold and listened "as Elvis quietly moaned."

BILL RAY

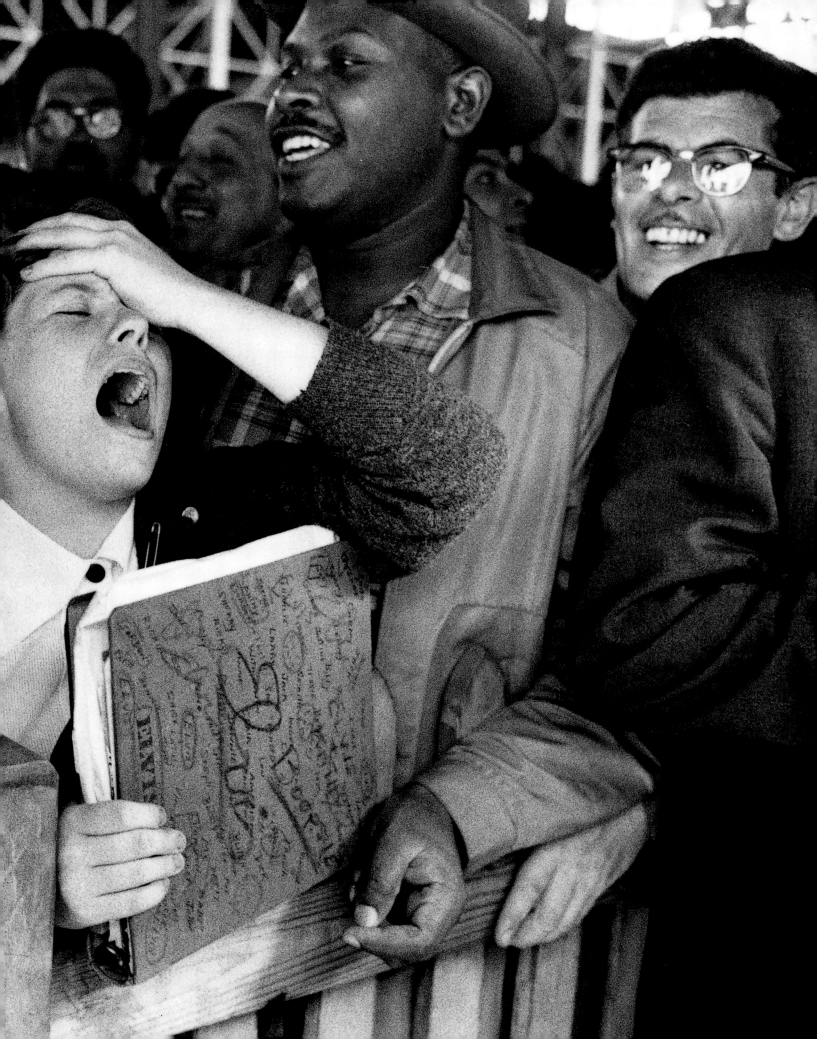

84

W HILE SERVING IN THE 3RD ARMORED DIVISION, ELVIS LIVED IN AN UNPRETENTIOUS HOUSE IN BAD NAUHEIM. A SIGN OUT FRONT READ AUTOGRAPHS BETWEEN 7:30 AND 8:30 P.M. LIVING WITH HIM WERE HIS FATHER, HIS GRANDMOTHER MINNIE MAE AND HIS FRIENDS RED WEST AND LAMAR FIKE. NONE OF THESE MEMPHIANS EVER REALLY GOT USED TO EUROPEAN LIFE: RED WAS CONSTANTLY BRAWLING IN BEER GARDENS AND MINNIE MAE'S HOUSEKEEPING BATTLES WITH THEIR LANDLORD, FRAU PIEPER, WERE ALMOST AS VIOLENT—ON ONE OCCASION, FRAU PIEPER GOT CLONKED WITH A BROOM HANDLE. ELVIS WAS A GOOD SOLDIER AND ADVANCED TO THE RANK OF SERGEANT, BUT, COMPARED WITH WHAT HE WAS USED TO, HIS LIFE WAS DEADLY DULL— AND IT WAS AT THIS TIME, FRIENDS SAID, HE BEGAN USING STIMULANTS.

BOTH ELVIS AND HIS FATHER, DESPERATE TO FILL THE VOID LEFT BY GLADYS, MET THEIR FUTURE BRIDES IN GERMANY, BUT TWO MORE DIFFERENT FEMALES CANNOT BE IMAGINED. DEE STANLEY WAS WORLDLY—IN FACT, SHE WAS MARRIED WHEN SHE STARTED DATING VERNON. PRISCILLA BEAULIEU WAS THE PICTURE OF INNOCENCE, A 14-YEAR-OLD IN A SAILOR SUIT, WHEN ELVIS FIRST LAID EYES ON HER. FOR SIX MONTHS, PRISCILLA AND ELVIS SPENT LONG EVENINGS IN HIS BEDROOM, TALKING INTIMATELY AND SMOOCHING PASSIONATELY. THE NIGHT BEFORE HE WAS TO RETURN TO THE STATES, SHE LATER WROTE, "I BEGGED HIM TO CONSUMMATE OUR LOVE, " BUT ELVIS DECLINED. SHE WAS TOO YOUNG, AND BESIDES, HE SAID, "I'M TORN WITH THE FEELINGS I HAVE FOR YOU." THE NEXT MORNING, AFTER LEADING MINNIE MAE TO HER CAR (FAR LEFT), PRISCILLA RODE WITH ELVIS TO THE AIRPORT (NEAR LEFT.) HE GAVE HER HIS COMBAT JACKET ("IT SHOWS YOU BELONG TO ME") AND TOLD HER TO WRITE HIM LETTERS ON PINK STATIONERY. "THEN HE DISAPPEARED. JUST LIKE THAT."

DESPITE HIS TENDER FAREWELL TO HIS FUTURE BRIDE, ELVIS WAS ALL BUSINESS LATER THAT AFTERNOON AT A FORT DIX PRESS CONFERENCE BEFORE SOME 200 REPORTERS. "I AM FOND OF PRISCILLA," HE SAID FIRMLY, "BUT I HAVE NO PLANS TO CALL OR WRITE HER. I DON'T JUST DATE SIXTEEN-YEAR-OLDS." (ACTUALLY, SHE WAS STILL 14.) PENCILS WIGGLED FEVERISHLY AS HE CHATTED WITH ACTRESSES NANCY SINATRA AND TINA LOUISE. "I BROUGHT TWO LACE SHIRTS AND A TELEGRAM GREETING FROM MY DAD," SAID SINATRA. "I BROUGHT MYSELF," SAID LOUISE (FAR RIGHT), LATER FAMOUS AS GINGER, THE RAVISHING MOVIE STAR, ON TV'S *GILLIGAN'S ISLAND*. (WHEN REPORTERS IN GERMANY TOLD PRISCILLA ABOUT ALL OF THIS, SHE "FELT SUDDENLY SICK," BUT ELVIS DID PHONE HER THREE WEEKS LATER.) HE HAD MUCH MORE THAN HIS LOVE LIFE TO THINK ABOUT. IN LESS THAN THREE WEEKS, HE WOULD RECEIVE $125,000 TO APPEAR ON THE *THE FRANK SINATRA TIMEX SHOW*. HE WAS PETRIFIED. HIS ONLY LIVE PERFORMANCE IN THE ARMY HAD OCCURRED WHEN DANCING GIRLS AT A PARIS NIGHTCLUB HAD PULLED HIM ONSTAGE. "FOR THE FRST TIME IN FIFTEEN MONTHS, I WAS IN FRONT OF AN AUDIENCE," HE SAID. "THEN IT FLEW ALL OVER ME, BOY— SUDDEN FEAR. I RECKON WHEN I GET IN FRONT OF THOSE CAMERAS I'M GOING TO SHAKE EVEN MORE THAN I DID BEFORE."

89

The Sinatra show went fine: The Chairman of the Board sang "Love Me Tender" and Elvis sang "Witchcraft." He was still on top, but adjusting to his new life was hard. He burned with anger over his father's marriage to Dee Stanley, declining to attend the wedding. He did his best to welcome Dee to Graceland with her sons ("I've always wanted a little brother, and now I have three"), but when she did a little redecorating without his permission, he tore down the curtains in a fury. His energy was now focused on Hollywood. "More than anything, I want to be an actor," he said. "The kind that stays around for a long time." His producer, Hal Wallis, claimed to regard him as a "genius" but, in his own words, "decided to take advantage of the situation" and cast Elvis in *G.I. Blues,* a mindless flick about a rock-and-roll soldier. "One longs to grip [Wallis] by the lapels," Elaine Dundy later wrote in *Elvis and Gladys,* "shake him, and snarl, 'So *this* is the way you treat your geniuses!'"

T WAS SO DAMNED AGGRAVATING. HE WAS

GOING THROUGH STACKS OF DEMO RECORDS

CHOOSING SONGS FOR HIS NEXT MOVIE

BUT HE HATED THEM ALL. HE PLACED EACH

ONE ON THE TURNTABLE, LISTENED TO A

FEW BARS, THEN YANKED IT OFF IN

DISGUST. FINALLY, HE FOUND ONE THAT

DIDN'T SEEM AS BAD AS THE REST AND

ASKED PRISCILLA TO LISTEN TO IT. "I

DON'T REALLY LIKE IT," SHE SAID. HE

EXPLODED WITH RAGE, HURLING A STACK OF

RECORDS IN HER FACE. THEN, FLOODED

WITH SHAME, HE TOOK HER IN HIS ARMS AND

APOLOGIZED. IT WAS SO DAMNED AGGRAVATING

"WHAT HAVE THEY DONE TO ELVIS?" THE NEW YORK *HERALD TRIBUNE* LAMENTED AFTER THE RELEASE OF *HARUM SCARUM*. IT WAS ELVIS'S FIFTEENTH FILM IN FIVE YEARS AND THOUGH, AS A VALENTINO FAN, HE'D BEGUN IT WITH HIGH HOPES, IT TURNED OUT TO BE PERHAPS HIS MOST EMBARRASSING VENTURE EVER. AFTER THE FILM WRAPPED, HE TIMIDLY TOLD A LIFE REPORTER HE WANTED "TO DO SOMETHING OF A DIFFERENT NATURE, SOMETHING THERE WOULD BE AN ACHIEVEMENT IN." BUT, COLONEL PARKER TOLD THE SAME REPORTER, "I DON'T THINK WE SHOULD EXPERIMENT WITH SOMETHING THAT'S MAKING A PROFIT." IN MANY THEATERS, *HARUM SCARUM* APPEARED ON A DOUBLE BILL WITH A JAPANESE FILM CALLED *GHIDRAH, THE THREE-HEADED MONSTER*; IT ALSO MADE MONEY HAND OVER FIST.

"THESE ARE PRESLEY PICTURES," AN MGM OFFICIAL TOLD *TIME* IN 1965. "THEY DON'T NEED TITLES. THEY COULD BE NUMBERED. THEY WOULD STILL SELL." IN FACT, THEY GROSSED MORE THAN $150 MILLION AT THE BOX OFFICE AND, EXCEPT FOR THE COST OF ELVIS HIMSELF, WERE RELATIVELY INEXPENSIVE TO PRODUCE. *HARUM SCARUM*, FOR INSTANCE, WAS SHOT IN 18 DAYS AND USED COSTUMES FROM *KISMET* AND A SET FROM CECIL B. DeMILLE'S *KING OF KINGS*. ELVIS MADE 31 MOVIES IN ALL (EXCLUDING DOCUMENTARIES), 27 OF THEM BETWEEN 1960 AND 1969. PICTURED HERE IS A POSTER OR LOBBY CARD FROM EACH ONE.

1956

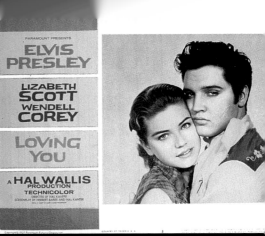

1957

961

1961

1962

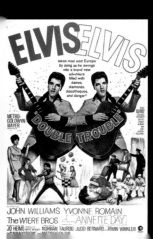

964

1964

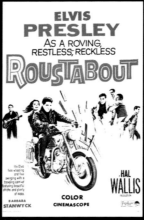

1964

1965

1965

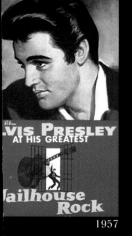
1957

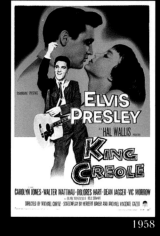
1958

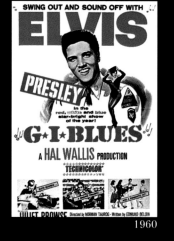
1960

1960

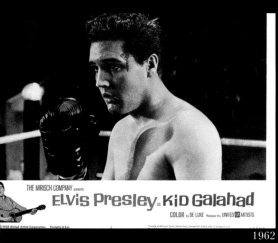
1962

1962

1963

1963

1965

1966

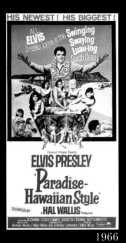
1966

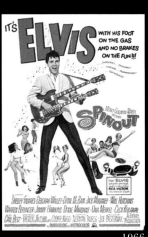
1966

1967

1968

1969

1969

1969

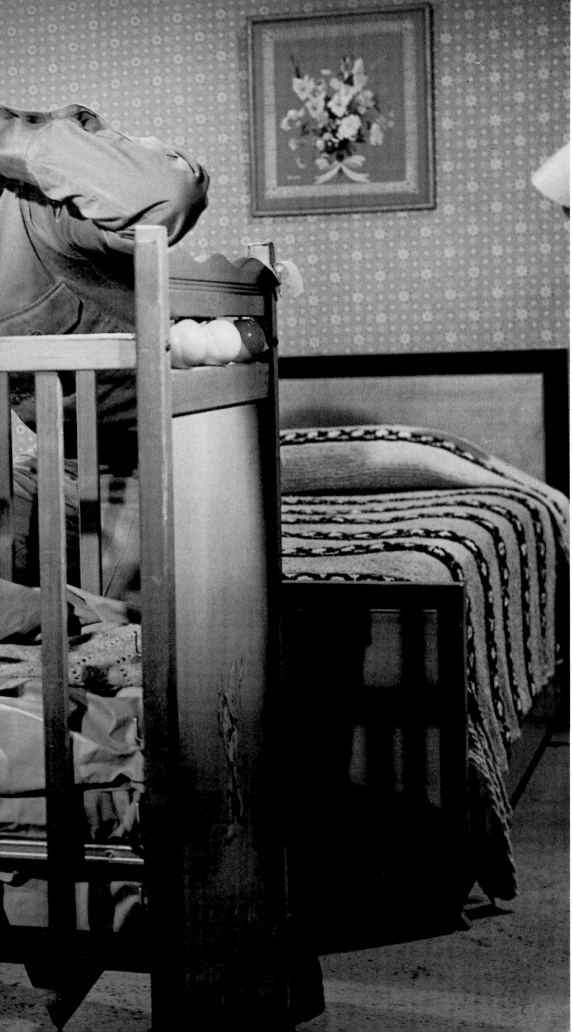

H E WOULD BE
A DREAM TO DIRECT,"
SAID GEORGE CUKOR,
WHO HAD DIRECTED,
AMONG OTHERS, TRACY,
HEPBURN, GARLAND,
GARBO, BERGMAN AND
BARRYMORE. "HE CAN
DO *ANYTHING*." THE
QUESTION IS: WHY
DIDN'T HE? "THE MAIN
REASON WAS HIS
INABILITY TO STAND UP
TO THE COLONEL,"
WROTE PRISCILLA,
AND MOST OF ELVIS'S
FRIENDS AND
ASSOCIATES AGREED.
"HE WOULDN'T STAND
UP BECAUSE THE
COLONEL WAS A
GREAT BUSINESSMAN,"
SAID RED WEST,
WHO WORKED ON 27
OF ELVIS'S FILMS
(INCLUDING *G.I.
BLUES*, LEFT). "NO ONE
IN ELVIS'S FAMILY
HAD A HEAD FOR
BUSINESS, AND HE WAS
AFRAID OF MAKING
A WRONG MOVE—IT
WAS TORTURE FOR
HIM." IT IS IMPORTANT
TO NOTE THAT PARKER
OFTEN BRAGGED OF
HIS ABILITY TO "SNOW"
PEOPLE, AND VETERAN
PRODUCER STEVE
BINDER WAS STRUCK
BY HIS "STRANGE,
HYPNOTIC, TOTAL
CONTROL OVER ELVIS."
THE LATE PHILIP
DUNNE, WHO DIRECTED
WILD IN THE COUNTRY,
ADDED BLUNTLY:
"WHAT I HAD AGAINST
PARKER WAS THAT
HE WAS A TASTELESS
MAN WHO HAD POWER
AND USED IT."

"THE CRITICS CAN SAY WHATEVER THEY WANT," SAID MOVIE SONGWRITER BEN WEISMAN. "THE BOTTOM LINE IS: THE PUBLIC LOVED HIS MOVIES!" INDEED, DESPITE THEIR POOR QUALITY, THERE WAS ALWAYS SOMETHING TO LOVE: GOOFY HUMOR, CAMPY SEXINESS, EVEN THE REASSURING PREDICTABILITY THESE STILLS REFLECT.

Jailhouse Rock

It Happened at the World's Fair

Wild in the Country

Flaming Star

Follow That Dream

Girls! Girls! Girls!

"I FEEL LIKE A GODDAMN IDIOT BREAKING INTO SONG WHEN I'M TALKING TO SOME CHICK ON A TRAIN," HE COMPLAINED TO PRISCILLA IN 1960. LITTLE DID HE KNOW THAT, SEVEN YEARS LATER, HIS ROLE IN *STAY AWAY, JOE* WOULD REQUIRE HIM TO SING TO A BULL NAMED DOMINIC.

Double Trouble

Girl Happy

Harum Scarum

Fun in Acapulco

Easy Come, Easy Go

Blue Hawaii

MUSIC WAS THE
BIGGEST CASUALTY OF
ELVIS'S FILM CAREER.
HE LABORED THROUGH
SUCH GROANERS AS
"QUEENIE WAHINE'S
PAPAYA," "YOGA IS AS
YOGA DOES" AND
"(THERE'S) NO ROOM
TO RHUMBA IN A SPORTS
CAR." "TERRIBLE
STUFF!" SHUDDERED
SCOTTY MOORE. "BUT
ELVIS DID EVERY
SONG TO THE VERY
BEST OF HIS ABILITY."

The Trouble with Girls

King Creole

G.I. Blues

Stay Away, Joe

Kid Galahad

Live a Little, Love a Little

FINALLY, IN 1969,
HE WENT PUBLIC,
ADMITTING TO BRITISH
JOURNALIST RAY
CONNOLLY THAT HE
WAS "ASHAMED" OF
SOME OF HIS MOVIES
AND THAT HE'D "BEEN
EXTREMELY UNHAPPY
WITH THAT SIDE OF
MY CAREER FOR SOME
TIME.... FROM NOW
ON," HE VOWED, "I'M
GOING TO PLAY SERIOUS
PARTS." BUT HE
NEVER ACTED AGAIN.

Speedway

Viva Las Vegas

Clambake

Loving You

Spinout

Change of Habit

ELVIS WOULD
SAY, 'O.K., IF WE'RE
GOING TO MAKE
THIS CRAP, SOMEHOW
WE'RE GOING TO HAVE
SOME FUN DOING IT,'"
RECALLED RED WEST.
CONSEQUENTLY,
THE MEMPHIS MAFIA
TURNED THE SETS
OF ELVIS'S MOVIES
INTO FRATERNITY
PARTIES. GROWN MEN
GIGGLED UPROARIOUSLY
OVER EXPLODING
FIRECRACKERS, WATER-
BALLOON FIGHTS AND
THE UNTYING OF BIKINI
TOPS. ONCE, WHILE
FILMING *CLAMBAKE*,
ELVIS GAVE BILL BIXBY
A PIE IN THE FACE.
FROM TIME TO TIME A
DIRECTOR OR A STUDIO
EXECUTIVE WOULD
COMPLAIN, BUT TO NO
AVAIL. "IT WAS HIS WAY
OF REBELLING," SAID
WEST. "HE HAD TO DO
SOMETHING TO KEEP
FROM GOING CRAZY."

RIENDS WHO HAD KNOWN HIM SINCE THE BEGINNING REMEMBERED A TIME WHEN THE SIGHT OF A PRETTY GIRL MADE ELVIS ACT "LIKE A KID WITH SIX PAIR OF FEET." ONCE WHILE SHOOTING *WILD IN THE COUNTRY*, HE RELAPSED INTO SELF-CONSCIOUSNESS WHEN AN ERUPTION OF BOILS EMERGED ON HIS HIND END. AS HE LAY NAKED IN HIS MOTEL SUITE, THE ACTRESS HOPE LANGE PAID HIM A VISIT. SHE DIDN'T ASK—SHE JUST LIFTED HIS SHEET AND HAD A LOOK. "WHOA, THERE!" HE CRIED, BLUSHING AND SNATCHING BACK THE SHEET. IT MAY HAVE BEEN THE LAST TIME HE EVER FELT EMBARRASSED. HOLLYWOOD'S HORDES OF BEAUTIFUL, WILLING WOMEN BASHED THE BASHFULNESS OUT OF HIM (AT RIGHT, HE NIBBLED JUDY TYLER'S FINGER ON THE SET OF *JAILHOUSE ROCK*). HE STILL HAD THE SAME CHARMING AW-SHUCKS-MA'AM POLITENESS, BUT, "IT WAS NO LONGER NATURAL," SAID ONE MEMPHIS MAFIOSO. "IT BECAME HIS LINE. . . . ONCE HE DISCOVERED HOW EASY IT WAS FOR HIM TO GET GIRLS, WE WERE ROUTING THEM THROUGH HIS BEDROOMS TWO AND SOMETIMES THREE A DAY."

FOR FIVE YEARS, WHILE HER MAN PLAYED HOLLYWOOD CASANOVA, PRISCILLA BEAULIEU TRAINED TO BE MRS. ELVIS. FROM THE TIME SHE MOVED INTO GRACELAND AT THE AGE OF 17, ELVIS EXPECTED HER TO BE ONE PART SERVANT, ONE PART SEX KITTEN, AND ONE PART NAIVE SCHOOLGIRL, OBLIVIOUS TO HIS WOMANIZING. BUT SHE STUCK IT OUT, AND ON MAY 1, 1967, THE KING, WEARING A DARK PAISLEY TUX, WED HIS QUEEN. "SHE WAS ABSOLUTELY PETRIFIED," SAID NEVADA SUPREME COURT JUDGE DAVID ZENOFF, WHO MARRIED THEM. AND ELVIS "WAS SO NERVOUS HE WAS ALMOST BAWLING."

As filming begins on *Viva Las Vegas,* Elvis begins a torrid affair with costar Ann-Margret. ("She's the female you," one friend tells him.) The film turns out to be one of Elvis's best, largely because of the magnetism between the stars. After his death, many of Elvis's friends will insist that it was she whom Elvis wanted to wed—and should have.

Elvis meets his mop-topped rivals when the Beatles stop by his Bel-Air, Calif., digs for a chat and a bit of a sing. Paul McCartney is amazed by Elvis's remote-control TV switch: "He was the first guy I ever saw who had one of those."

Elvis purchases the Circle G Ranch near Walls, Miss., for about $300,000. For a while he and the Memphis Mafia enjoy dressing up like cowboys and riding the range, but before the end of the year, he will grow bored with the place.

A car is set ablaze on the Graceland grounds, and the following day Elvis beats up a yardman, Troy Ivy. The public begins to get the sense that all is not right in the Kingdom.

JULY 1963   **AUGUST 1965**   **FEBRUARY 1967**   **SEPTEMBER 1967**

ELVIS HAD
LITTLE TO SMILE
ABOUT IN THE MONTHS
BEFORE WINGING HIS
WAY TO PALM SPRINGS
WITH HIS BRIDE. HE
HAD NOT APPEARED IN
CONCERT SINCE
MARCH OF 1961, AND
HIS CAREER WAS
AT AN ALL-TIME LOW.
TO MAKE MATTERS
WORSE, JUST AS
HE WAS TO BEGIN
FILMING *CLAMBAKE*
(ABOUT TWO MONTHS
BEFORE THIS PICTURE
WAS TAKEN), HE
HAD TRIPPED ON AN
ELECTRICAL CORD,
WHACKED HIS HEAD
ON A BATHTUB
AND SUFFERED A
CONCUSSION. IT WAS
WONDERFUL TO
FORGET ALL THIS FOR
A WHILE. AFTER THE
HONEYMOON HE TOOK
PRISCILLA TO HIS
RANCH IN MISSISSIPPI,
WHERE THEY STAYED
IN A TRAILER. THEN,
NINE MONTHS TO THE
DAY AFTER THEIR
MARRIAGE, SHE GAVE
BIRTH TO THEIR
FIRST AND ONLY
CHILD, LISA MARIE.

ON A SUMMER DAY IN 1968 HE STOOD IN FRONT OF AN

UNOPEN BAR ON L.A.'S SUNSET STRIP. STEVE BINDER WAS

RIGHT: HE WAS UNRECOGNIZABLE; PEOPLE WERE PASSING BY

WITHOUT GIVING HIM A SECOND LOOK. THE NBC PRODUCER

HAD DARED ELVIS TO SHOW HIMSELF IN PUBLIC, AND

THERE WAS NO GETTING AROUND IT, ELVIS WAS AS COLD

AS WEEK-OLD CORN BREAD. SOMETHING HAD TO BE DONE.

COMING BACK

SHEER TERROR. THAT WAS WHAT ELVIS FELT BEFORE HIS 1968 COMEBACK SPECIAL ON NBC. THE REASON: IT WOULD BE TAPED BEFORE A LIVE AUDIENCE. "FOR NEARLY TEN YEARS, I HAVE BEEN KEPT AWAY FROM THE PUBLIC," HE CONFIDED TO HIS PRODUCER. "AND THE ONE THING I LOVED WAS PERFORMING. BUT I'M NOT SURE THEY'RE GONNA *LIKE* ME NOW." ELVIS PULLED OUT ALL THE STOPS: HE DIETED, HE REHEARSED, HE WORE A BLACK LEATHER BIKER'S OUTFIT. ELVIS NEVER LOOKED BETTER. AND AS HE JAMMED WITH SCOTTY AND D.J. (WHO BEAT OUT ALL HIS DRUM PARTS ON THE TOP OF A GUITAR CASE), HE NEVER SOUNDED BETTER.

I'VE GOT TO GET BACK IN FRONT OF THE PUBLIC," AN ELATED ELVIS TOLD COLONEL PARKER AFTER THE COMEBACK SPECIAL. ON JULY 31, 1969, HE PLAYED HIS FIRST LIVE DATE IN ALMOST A DECADE. THE AUDIENCE AT THE INTERNATIONAL HOTEL IN LAS VEGAS INCLUDED CARY GRANT, FATS DOMINO, HENRY MANCINI AND SAMMY DAVIS JR. *ROLLING STONE* CALLED HIS PERFORMANCE "SUPERNATURAL." FOR THE REST OF HIS LIFE, HE TRIED TO SURPASS IT (AS AT RIGHT, CIRCA 1972).

ATTENDING AN ELVIS CONCERT IN THE '70S WAS LIKE ROLLING THE DICE IN A VEGAS CASINO: ANYTHING FROM A JACKPOT TO A CRAP-OUT WAS POSSIBLE. HIS JUMPSUITS WERE SPECTACULAR (RIGHT)—BUT IF HIS WEIGHT WAS OUT OF CONTROL, HE WAS LIABLE TO BUST HIS SEAMS, AS HE DID ONE NIGHT IN PONTIAC, MICH., BEFORE 62,000 ASTONISHED FANS. HIS TCB (TAKIN' CARE OF BUSINESS) BAND WAS ALMOST ALWAYS SPLENDID— BUT IF HE HAD GOBBLED TOO MANY DRUGS BEFORE COMING ONSTAGE, HE WAS LIABLE TO FORGET HIS LYRICS OR BURST INTO FITS OF GIGGLING. HE WAS WALKING A TIGHTROPE. IN RETROSPECT, IT IS INCREDIBLE THAT HE WAS ABLE TO KEEP HIS BALANCE AS LONG AS HE DID.

Elvis writes President Nixon a rambling letter, requesting a visit and a federal narc's badge. He says he wants to fight "drug abuse and communist brainwashing techniques." Elvis gets his meeting— and his badge—but subsequently turns down Nixon's invitation to play the White House.

A live performance at the Honolulu International Center is beamed to television audiences in 36 countries around the world. As many as 1.5 billion people will tune in. When it's all over, Elvis—who had dropped 20 pounds for the show—is so exhausted, he sleeps for 24 hours.

Elvis holds discussions with Barbra Streisand at the Las Vegas Hilton on the possibility of costarring with her in *A Star Is Born.* Elvis wants desperately to do it, but the Colonel later turns thumbs down.

He purchases a Convair 880 jet for $250,000, names it the *Lisa Marie,* then spends $750,000 customizing it with a purple carpet, queen-size bed and gold bathroom fixtures.

ELVIS'S LAST HOPE FOR SURVIVAL LAY WITH HIS FAMILY, WHOM HE TRULY LOVED. BUT DRUGS AND HIS PHILANDERING DROVE PRISCILLA AWAY FROM HIM, AND DRUGS AND WORK KEPT HIM FROM GIVING LISA MARIE THE ATTENTION SHE DESERVED. ALTHOUGH THIS 1971 PORTRAIT FOUND THE FAMILY IN A RARE OPTIMISTIC MOOD—ELVIS WAS BACK ON TOP AND PRISCILLA WILLING TO MAKE ANOTHER GO OF IT—THEY SEPARATED THE FOLLOWING YEAR.

A group of investors, including his physician George "Dr. Nick" Nichopoulos and longtime Memphis Mafioso "Diamond" Joe Esposito, convince Elvis to invest in a scheme to build racquetball courts. The following year, they will wind up suing him over this faltering venture—though Esposito will remain his employee and Dr. Nick his doctor until Elvis's death.

Jerry Lee Lewis, with whom Elvis had so enjoyed jamming at Sun Studios 20 years before, is arrested in the wee hours of the morning in front of Graceland's gates. "The Killer," as Lewis calls himself, is drunk, disorderly and armed with a .38 derringer. "I was really rockin' that night," he will later laugh.

After nearly five years as his lover, Linda Thompson moves out of Graceland. She is tired of "baby-sitting" Elvis, she says, and worried that he is killing himself.

Furious at being abruptly fired after years of faithful service, Memphis Mafia members Dave Hebler and Red and Sonny West publish *Elvis: What Happened?,* which details their former boss's drug use, sex life and obsession with guns. Elvis sees the book in galleys and wails: "My life is over. I'm a dead man."

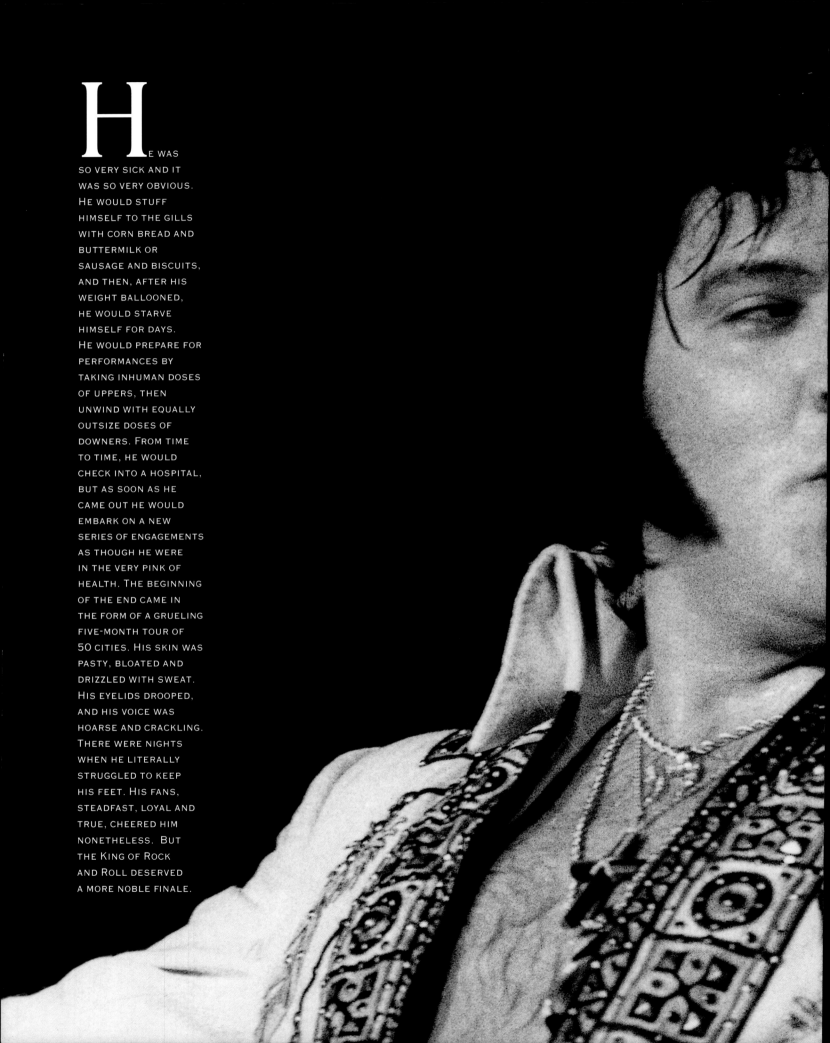

H

E WAS SO VERY SICK AND IT WAS SO VERY OBVIOUS. HE WOULD STUFF HIMSELF TO THE GILLS WITH CORN BREAD AND BUTTERMILK OR SAUSAGE AND BISCUITS, AND THEN, AFTER HIS WEIGHT BALLOONED, HE WOULD STARVE HIMSELF FOR DAYS. HE WOULD PREPARE FOR PERFORMANCES BY TAKING INHUMAN DOSES OF UPPERS, THEN UNWIND WITH EQUALLY OUTSIZE DOSES OF DOWNERS. FROM TIME TO TIME, HE WOULD CHECK INTO A HOSPITAL, BUT AS SOON AS HE CAME OUT HE WOULD EMBARK ON A NEW SERIES OF ENGAGEMENTS AS THOUGH HE WERE IN THE VERY PINK OF HEALTH. THE BEGINNING OF THE END CAME IN THE FORM OF A GRUELING FIVE-MONTH TOUR OF 50 CITIES. HIS SKIN WAS PASTY, BLOATED AND DRIZZLED WITH SWEAT. HIS EYELIDS DROOPED, AND HIS VOICE WAS HOARSE AND CRACKLING. THERE WERE NIGHTS WHEN HE LITERALLY STRUGGLED TO KEEP HIS FEET. HIS FANS, STEADFAST, LOYAL AND TRUE, CHEERED HIM NONETHELESS. BUT THE KING OF ROCK AND ROLL DESERVED A MORE NOBLE FINALE.

117

HE WAS SAID TO BE SUFFERING FROM GLAUCOMA, HYPERTENSION, AN ENLARGED HEART, CLOGGED ARTERIES AND A TWISTED COLON. HE WAS PROBABLY TAKING PERCODAN (A NARCOTIC PAINKILLER), DEXEDRINE (A STIMULANT), AMYTAL (A BARBITURATE), QUAALUDE (A HYPNOTIC SEDATIVE), DILAUDID (ANOTHER PAINKILLER), BIPHETAMINE (AN AMPHETAMINE) AND THE DEVIL ONLY KNEW WHAT ELSE. STILL, WHEN THE END DID COME, IT WAS A SHOCK. "I WILL NEVER FORGET THE LOOKS OF TOTAL DISBELIEF ON THE FACES THAT LINED BOTH SIDES OF ELVIS PRESLEY BOULEVARD FOR THE FUNERAL PROCESSION," SAID SAM PHILLIPS. "IT SEEMED AS THOUGH EACH PERSON STOOD COMPLETELY ALONE."

1977

AUGUST 16

OW MUCH IS HE MISSED? SHORTLY AFTER HIS DEATH, A FEMALE ELVIS

MPERSONATOR HAD PLASTIC SURGERY TO MAKE HER ACT MORE

ONVINCING. SOME 15 YEARS LATER, A JAPANESE MAN PAID MORE THAN

IVE MILLION YEN FOR HIS ELVIS REGALIA AND CONDUCTED AN EXHAUSTIVE

TUDY OF THE PRESLEY KI (JAPANESE FOR "SPIRIT") EN ROUTE TO WINNING

HE SIXTH ANNUAL INTERNATIONAL ELVIS IMPERSONATORS CONTEST. BY

HE BEGINNING OF 1995, TWO GROUPS OF SKYDIVING IMPERSONATORS,

HE "FLYING ELVISES" AND THE "FLYING ELVI," WERE SUING EACH

OTHER IN FEDERAL COURT. *THAT* IS HOW MUCH HE IS MISSED.

LIVES

ELVIS

UNABATED SINCE HIS PASSING. EVEN THE RICHARD NIXON PRESIDENTIAL LIBRARY IN YORBA LINDA, CALIF., HAS GOTTEN INTO THE ACT, OFFERING A $45 WRISTWATCH DECORATED WITH A PORTRAIT OF THE FORMER PRESIDENT SHAKING HANDS WITH THE ONETIME KING. AT A RECENT BUTTERFIELD & BUTTERFIELD AUCTION, A PIECE OF BROKEN TREE LIMB FROM GRACELAND WAS SOLD FOR $747.50. BUT THE MARKET DOES SEEM TO HAVE SETTLED DOWN A BIT SINCE 1979, WHEN MEMPHIS DRY CLEANER WILLIAM RES CARWILE HAD ELVIS'S ORIGINAL CRYPT AT FOREST HILL CEMETERY CARVED INTO 44,000 PIECES (ELVIS'S BODY HAD BEEN MOVED TO GRACELAND, WHERE IT LIES TODAY) AND OFFERED THEM FOR SALE AT $80 A CHUNK.

(PREVIOUS PAGE) HIS NAME IS EL VEZ AND HE IS NOT, HE SAYS, SO MUCH AN "ELVIS IMPERSONATOR" AS AN "ELVIS INTERPRETER." HE REFRIES PRESLEY AND SERVES HIM UP *CON SALSA* WITH SUCH FIERY FARE AS "YOU AIN'T NOTHIN' BUT A CHIHUAHUA." AMONG SENOR VEZ'S MANY COSTUMES IS A PURPLE CRUSHED VELVET JUMPSUIT EMBROIDERED WITH AN IMAGE OF THE VIRGIN OF GUADALUPE.

ALMOST AS SOON AS HE WAS REPORTED DEAD, PEOPLE BEGAN SWEARING THEY'D SEEN ELVIS WALKING AMONG US, AS ALIVE AS ON THE DAY HE WAS BORN. HE WAS FIRST OBSERVED AT FELPAUSCH FOOD CENTER IN VICKSBURG, MICH.; THEN AT A BURGER KING IN KALAMAZOO; THEN AT A BAR IN RIVERHEAD, N.Y.; THEN AT A CARNIVAL IN DENTON, TEX; AND SO ON. IN 1991 A YANKELOVICH POLL FOUND THAT APPROXIMATELY ONE OUT OF SIX AMERICANS BELIEVED ELVIS MIGHT STILL BE ALIVE. NONSENSE, SAYS MARY JENKINS (LEFT). SHE WAS A GRACELAND DOMESTIC FOR 26 YEARS AND SHE KNOWS. BESIDES, SHE SAYS, NOT LONG AFTER ELVIS DIED, HIS SPIRIT CAME TO HER IN A DREAM AND ASKED PERMISSION TO DROP BY FOR A REST. "AND I SAID, 'WELL, YOU KNOW YOU'RE *ALWAYS* WELCOME.' AND I FIXED THE ROOM FOR HIM IN THE BACK OF MY HOUSE, AND HIS SPIRIT MOVED ON IN." JENKINS, AND THE SPIRIT OF ELVIS, NOW LIVE IN THE MEMPHIS HOME PRESLEY BOUGHT FOR HER IN 1974.

More tourists visit Graceland than any other home in America except the White House—700,000 last year alone. They come to see not only the mansion but also Elvis's glittering jumpsuits (in styles ranging from "American Eagle" to "Inca Gold Leaf"); his fleet of automobiles (from Stutzes to go-carts); his bizarre arsenal of guns (including a gold Pietro Beretta pistol); and even, alas, his well-thumbed copy of the *Physician's Desk Reference* (an encyclopedia of prescription drugs). The anniversary of Elvis's death in mid-August is a special time at Graceland, a time when the grounds overflow with the people who love him most. They know that some make sport of their devotion, but they don't care. They come to light candles in Elvis's memory and sing the gospel songs he loved. "Take my hand, precious Lord," they sing, "lead me home."

"HUSH, LITTLE BABY, DON'T YOU CRY.

YOU KNOW YOUR DADDY'S BOUND TO DIE.

BUT ALL MY TRIALS, LORD, WILL SOON BE OVER."